Negotiating Spain and Catalonia

Competing Narratives of National Identity

Fernando León Solís

intellect™
Bristol, UK
Portland, OR, USA

Published in Paperback in UK in 2003 by
Intellect Books, PO Box 862, Bristol BS99 1DE, UK

Published in Paperback in USA in 2003 by
Intellect Books, ISBS, 920 NE 58th Ave. Suite 300, Portland, Oregon 97213-3786, USA

Cover Image: Martín González
Copy Editor: Holly Spradling

A catalogue record for this book is available from the British Library

ISBN 1-84150-077-1

Printed in Great Britain by Antony Rowe Ltd, Eastbourne.

CONTENTS

ABOUT THE AUTHOR

Fernando León Solís was born in Montoro in the Southern Spanish region of Andalusia. He studied English Language and Literature at Granada University and was awarded a PhD at Glasgow Caledonian University. He is now a Lecturer in Spanish at the University of Paisley in Scotland.

ACKNOWLEDGEMENTS

This book would not have been possible without the support of Glasgow Caledonian University, who provided the necessary funds for the completion of my PhD thesis on which this book is based. I am particularly grateful to Professor Hugh O'Donnell for his invaluable intellectual aid at all the stages of this book. I also feel gratitude to the University of Paisley for the material support received.

I owe a special debt of gratitude to Carlos Viegas, Gillian Pencovitch, Rosa Millán and John Scott for their friendly support; to Martín González for the design of the cover of this book; and to my brothers, sisters and parents, for their love and kindness.

To my parents, Isabel Solís and
Manuel León

INTRODUCTION

Controversial Identities

What is Spanish identity? What does being Spanish mean? If you follow the stereotype, one ready answer could be 'being Spanish means being passionate'. And indeed, Spanish companies have used this idea of passion and excitement in life in order to promote their products. Take, for example, the car manufacturer *SEAT*, which, although now owned by the German Volkswagen, has retained its 'Spanish identity' in its marketing campaigns. At the end of the adverts for all its products under the *SEAT* logo you can read the words 'Auto emoción' (meaning 'car emotion' but also 'self emotion'). A recent advert for the Spanish lager *San Miguel* being shown in British cinemas plays with the same idea – this time the reading is 'Spanish Passion for Life'.

Another concept Spanish companies like playing with, is that of a Spain somehow different from the rest of the European continent. The *San Miguel* advert mentioned above shows clips of Spanish people enjoying themselves during popular *fiestas* and also of women dressed up in the Muslim fashion, thus distancing Spain from the rest of Europe. And not only have companies used the idea of 'difference' to promote Spain, the Ministry of Tourism during the Francoist Regime came up with the slogan 'Spain is different' with the aim of converting Spain into an attractive country for not being the same as the rest of Europe. This construct of Spain as different from Europe also implied a single image of the country as characterized by bullfighters, flamenco dancers and gypsies.

The cases mentioned above refer to the promotion abroad of Spanish products or of Spain itself as a tourist destination. But how are these images of passion, emotion and difference received within Spain? If you approach this book already having some knowledge of Spanish culture you will be aware of the clear unease with these conceptions of national identity amongst many groups within Spain. You will also be aware of the fact that there is not really just one national image with which the majority of Spaniards identify. There are many different ideologically and territorially based conceptions of the country.

The strength of the ideological divisions is epitomized by the Manichean and almost mythological struggle between 'The Two Spains' (*Las dos Españas*) – the conservative and the liberal. Two groups that fight 'for the appropriation of the identity of the nation' (Morón Arroyo, 1996: 180), and whose strong opposition has been pointed out (rather simplistically, one might say) as the reason for the breakout of the Spanish Civil War (1936–1939). This divide has haunted Spanish society for so long and with such intensity that bringing it to an end was one of the greatest aims of the 1978 Constitution of the new democracy after the death of Franco. About Spanish identity, the discourse of 'liberal Spain' would argue that since Franco promoted the 'difference' between Spain and the rest of Europe, all the traces of that difference should disappear. For this discourse, being the same as other Europeans should be the main objective of Spaniards. And this identification with Europe implies that reason and moderation, not passion and emotion, should be the major components of Spanish identity. The discourse of conservative Spain (many times called 'Eternal Spain' – *La España Eterna*) is more in line with those traditional images associated with Spain which tend to establish a difference within the European context.

In peripheral regions such as Galicia, the Basque Country or Catalonia (with their own different languages and what many regard as their own culture altogether different from the rest of Spain), the association of Spain with passion, emotion, bullfighters and gypsies is also challenged on a daily basis. Amongst these peripheral regions, this book will concentrate on Catalonia and it will show how Catalans tend to see themselves as hardworking, moderate, responsible, thoughtful; that is, as characterized by an identity driven by reason and not by passion. It is not uncommon for Catalans to describe themselves as the only true Europeans in Spain. They are not different from the rest of Europe, they would say, they *are* and always *have been* a part of Europe. At the same time, they would argue, they are indeed different from the rest of Spain, regarded as a multi-cultural and multi-lingual state with no legitimate right to promote a single national identity for the whole of the country.

The debate on national identity has, of course, political implications regarding conceptions of the structure of the State. On the grounds of linguistic and cultural diversity, many Catalans advocate a federal or co-federal arrangement for Spain where regions have maximum autonomy. The opposite trend supports a unified and more centralized organization of the country. The strength of this struggle between centre and periphery has led some authors to argue that, 'Spanish history ... can be understood as a permanent tension between the pull towards centralization (centripetal) and the push towards fragmentation (centrifugal)' (Ucelay da Cal,

1996: 32). Perhaps foregrounding the politico-territorial controversy as the only driving force of Spanish history is somewhat exaggerated, but it can be rightly regarded as one of the deepest and most delicate problems which has prevented the emergence of an integrating national identity (Labanyi, 1995: 407).

This debate on Spanishness, Catalanicity, and the role of Catalonia in the whole of Spain, will be looked into in this book, which proposes a narrative study of four main competing discourses of Spanish and Catalan national identities as disseminated in the Spanish press in the period between 1993 and 1996 and, more briefly, after the 2000 elections. It shows how in times of political tension and friction between the all-Spanish parties and the peripheral nationalisms, these four versions of Spanish and Catalan identities can contradict each other and become radically opposed. Indeed, as will be seen, the relationship between them can reach the apocalyptic tones of a war. However, when the political circumstances calm down, those clashing constructions can be modified, and even be merged. In that sense, this study makes good Schlesinger's observation that national identity should be considered not as a static concept but as one that is constantly being redefined; that is, as a 'continually reconstructed category' (1991: 173) which must be regarded as within 'a determinate set of social relations' (*ibid*).

The book is divided into four chapters. Chapter 1 deals thoroughly with the following questions: what are these four discourses, what are their main media outlets, and what makes these periods of time so particular? For introductory purposes, let's touch briefly on those points.

Four Discourses

First of all, a working definition of discourse. In this book, discourse will be understood as the site of intersection between ideology and language; or, in other words, as broad ideological and linguistic parameters used by writers (in the case of the written media) and offered to the readers as a manner of looking at and talking about particular topics, objects and processes. According to this definition, the discourse of Catalanism, for example, refers to the language use of Catalanist thinkers or politicians, but also to the ideologies propagated by them. This is the conception of discourse of Blain *et al.* who use the term 'in a flexible sense of talking about or constructing ... versions of reality that are ideological' (Blain *et al.*, 1993: 4).

I have identified two main all-Spanish discourses (categorized along the lines of 'The Two Spains' seen above) and two Catalanist discourses. The conservative and unitarian Spain maintains a discourse which promotes a centralized vision of the country and a concept of national identity which is not only at times close to essentialism but also grudgingly accepts regional differences. The political party more akin to such discourse is the centre–right party Partido Popular. I will investigate this discourse mainly through the Madrid daily *Abc*.

The liberal Spain is more at ease with the concept of devolved powers to the regions, and 'modernity' and 'Europeanism' are the values that more clearly shape their concept of Spanish identity. In the political spectrum, this liberal Spain is close to the centre–left PSOE (Partido Socialista Obrero Español). I have studied this discourse through *El País*, which can be regarded as one of its main media outlets.

The two Catalanist discourses have been called 'differential' and 'disjunctive'. Both have a clear common axiom: Catalonia is a nation. However, they differ from each other on their conception of the place of Catalonia and her national identity within the all-Spanish framework. For the 'differential discourse', Spain might be regarded as a problematical political structure needing some radical reforms, but Catalonia is as an integral part of it. For this discourse, as long as Spain is constituted as a multi-lingual and multi-cultural space, or as 'a nation of nations', Catalonia will fit in the structure. This is the most popular discourse in Catalonia. It is the official line of Convèrgencia i Unió (CiU), the nationalist coalition that has ruled the Catalan Parliament throughout the whole of the democratic period. I have studied this discourse as disseminated mainly by the Barcelona daily *La Vanguardia*.

The disjunctive discourse takes a more radical stance: Spain and Catalonia are two different historical, sociological and identity realities and should be regarded as separate. Esquerra Republicana de Catalunya (ERC), Partit per la Independencia (PI), and less importantly, the more radical factions of CiU, are the political bastions of this trend. The Barcelona newspaper *Avui* will be looked into as a media outlet for the study of this discourse.

Chapter 1 will also briefly deal with the historical relevance of these four discourses, and will show how the national question in Spain, and the problem of national identity has haunted Spanish political life for centuries. It must be noted, however, that it does not intend to be a thorough historical review, but a brief introduction to the issue.

A list of acronyms of political parties is provided in the appendix.

The Period of Study: 1993–1996 and Beyond

Chapter 1 also answers in full the question 'why study this period in particular?' Here it will suffice to note that in the 1993 elections, after losing the overall majority they had enjoyed in the previous two terms, the PSOE sought the collaboration of the moderate Catalanists of Convergència i Unió in central government. This political agreement caused indignation in the centre–right main opposition party Partido Popular (PP) and their supporting media, mainly the Madrid daily *Abc*. They focused their attacks on the supposedly illegitimate collaboration of the Socialists with a coalition party accused of aiming at dismantling the State, political blackmail and opportunism.

This political atmosphere brought to the fore and radicalized discourses of national identity in the whole of Spain. In the all-Spanish liberal media, the idea of the existence of two Spains clashing with each other and with totally different identities was brought back to life. In the Catalan political field and media, the conviction of Catalonia and Spain as two separate entities with different identities, gained strength. The relationship between discourses reached bellicose tones.

This situation went on at least until the aftermath of the 1996 general elections: it was then the PP that won the elections, but due to the absence of an overall majority, they needed the collaboration of the Catalanists to form a government. That is, the circumstances took an about-turn. After a long process of negotiation, the bad blood between the PP and CiU gave way to an agreement. This agreement and collaboration of an all-Spanish centre–right with the moderate Catalanists were regarded by many as a 'historical revolution' (Sahagún, 2001: 378), due mainly to the radically opposed views of both parties on the structure of the Spanish state: centralist and co-federal, respectively. This pact reduced the political tension. Accordingly, the emphasis on difference between 'The Two Spains' and between Catalonia and Spain gave way to a very civilized consensus and common ground.

In 2000 the PP obtained its first overall majority. Although CiU was not anymore needed to form a government, the Catalanists maintained their support for the right-wing party. After this second agreement between the PP and CiU the territorial tension abated even more. However, the friction was not totally dispelled in this period of relative calm. The Catalanist daily *Avui*, as will be seen, established the exception.

Two Analyses

The constructions of national identities and their modifications through time will be the focus of study of this book. However, it is important to note that this is not an analysis of the subject using the instruments of political theory. It is rather a very practical investigation of the subject carried out, through the analysis of texts emblematic not only of each discourse, but also of the degree of competition with other discourses. These two analyses are organized in two case studies, which will take up the whole of chapters 2 and 3. Chapter 2, entitled 'The Game of the Nations: Football and Identity', will be dealing with the construction of Spanish and Catalan identities in the coverage and interpretation of the performance of the Spanish national football team during the '94 USA Football World Cup.

After introducing the origin and general features of the sporting aspects of the four discourses of national identity, the chapter concentrates on the study of the way in which such discourses competed among themselves in order to establish their own constructions of national identity. It shows how, against a background of political turmoil due to the attacks on the political pact between PSOE and CiU, these discourses interacted with each other in a mode which was 'agonistic' – that is, implicated in a process where 'to speak is to fight' (Lyotard, 1984: 10); or 'dialogic', to use Bakhtin's words (1981).

In that 'dialogue' or 'fight' between discourses, the images of Spain and its football team produced by newspapers with different ideologies were almost opposite. For example, the more conservative and centralist Madrid daily *Abc* proposed an image of Spain and its national team that was almost poetic by virtue of the use of 'extrahistorical language, a language far removed from the petty rounds of everyday life' (1981: 331), to use Bakhtin's definition of poetic style. For their part, liberal, differential and disjunctive discourse were closer to the 'art of prose' in their being close to an idea of 'languages as historically concrete and living things ... [their] deliberate feeling for the historical and social concreteness of living discourse, as well as its relativity, a feeling for its participation in historical becoming and in social struggle' (Bakhtin, 1981: 331).

Let's exemplify this point. Whereas for *Abc* the Spanish football team was almost invariably 'the National Team', for the Catalan writer and journalist Vázquez Montalbán, writing in the more liberal *El País* (in an article that will be fully analysed below), the team was 'The Team of The Autonomies' – the Autonomies being the 17 autonomous regions in which Spain was structured after the highly centralized Francoist state. That is, for *Abc*, the team was the representative of a nation, with all the sentimental and eternal connotations of the national concept. Vázquez Montalbán, however, constructed the team as the inapt representative of a rather more prosaic administrative structure shaped by 17 administrative entities.

These two poetic and prosaic constructions had a further implication. Whereas the Spanish 'nation' of *Abc* depicted a united country; with his reference to the Autonomies, Vázquez Montalbán stripped the sporting symbol of Spain off its eternal connotations and emphasized the lack of a solid national identity for the whole of the country. This lack of a national unity and identity was at times strongly constructed by references to the myth of The Two Spains.

The analysis in chapter 2 also includes an epilogue where I discuss the changes in the different discourses and the way they interacted after the relative 'territorial' calm brought about by the pacts between the PP and CiU, after the 1996 and the 2000 general elections. In that epilogue it will be clear that the two opposing Spains all but disappeared and most newspapers attempted a common definition of the country.

The shift from opposition to mutual understanding is also clear in chapter 3, which studies the process of negotiation towards the political pact between Partido Popular and Convergència i Unió after the 1996 general election as represented by the Catalan daily *La Vanguardia*. It is entitled 'Catalonia: Victim and Redeemer of Spain', and analyses the narrative strategy displayed by the Catalan newspaper *La Vanguardia* (close to the Catalan nationalist coalition CiU) with the aim of re-working the relationship between Spain and Catalonia and their constructed identities in order to legitimize the pact between the conservative Spanish party PP and CiU – generally regarded as 'political enemies' right up until the 1996 elections. From a relationship of confrontation, the two parties would reach a common ground thanks to the self-assigned redeeming role of the Catalanists. This agreement was also constructed in national terms: thanks to the role of Catalonia, Spain was redeemed and transformed into a place where Catalonia can fit in. The epilogue to this chapter will also analyse (albeit more briefly) the justification of the second agreement with the PP proposed by *La Vanguardia* after the 2000 elections. It will show how the spirit of collaboration and good harmony between the PP and CiU was reflected in the emphasis on the common ground between Spain and Catalonia.

Some Theoretical Points:

<u>Hegemony and Resistance</u>

It is clear from these two summaries that the subject matters of the two chapters, sport and politics, are different. However, they do not constitute isolated analyses. The variation is on purpose: I have attempted to demonstrate that the struggle for establishment of questions of national identity can take different forms in various cultural fields and still be interrelated, since they play a similar role in the broader socio-political scene. In this sense, the Gramscian concept of hegemony is central. For Gramsci, hegemony is the cultural, intellectual and moral leadership, which replaces 'domination' as the form of social and political struggle.

As Strinati points out, 'the [Gramscian] concept of hegemony can be applied to a wide range of social struggles' (Strinati, 2000: 174). This notion opens up the field of analysis of ideology to areas of cultural life such as popular culture, including sport. In chapter 2 it will be seen how the performance of the Spanish national football team (despite its apparent apolitical nature) can constitute the basic material for the generation of discourses which are totally involved in the processes whereby conceptions of the Spanish state and notions of national identity are defined[1].

Furthermore, the idea of hegemony presupposes conflict but also implies the notion of management of conflict: the idea that 'a certain compromise equilibrium should be formed' (Gramsci, 1971: 161). It also implies a two-way struggle whereby hegemonic discourses are fought back by counter-hegemonic ones by means of strategies of contestation, resignification, negotiation, and accommodation. How do these strategies work in the analyses? Chapter 2 in particular will show how the process of contestation and resignification of competing discourses is carried out by introducing the 'words of the others' and their values in one's own discourse. It will also be seen that this reproduction of the others' words is most of the time ironic and even parodic, with the ultimate aim of presenting rival discourses as illegitimate.

These strategies used in the struggle for hegemony will also be evident in the study of the media representation of the pact between Partido Popular and Convergència i Unió after the 1996 elections: the Catalanists, assisted by *La Vanguardia*, had to negotiate their own discourse in order to justify a kind of political action that had been long frowned upon beforehand – without accepting, of course, accusations of having conceded. As will be seen, the triumphant interpretation of events (which established that the PP and the whole of Spain had been transformed thanks to the Catalanists) met resistance even within *La Vanguardia*.

The Narrative Approach

There is a further common point between the two analyses: in both of them, national identities are expressed in narrative form. The universality of narratives in all fields, including politics and media discourse, has been made evident by many authors. As Barthes points out in his *Introduction to the Structural Analysis of Narratives*,

> the narratives of the world are numberless ... narrative is present in myth, legend, fable, tale, novella, epic, history, tragedy, drama, comedy, mime, painting ... stain glass windows, cinema, comics, news item, conversation ... narrative is present in every age, in every place, in every society ... narrative ... is simply there, like life itself (Barthes, 1987: 79).

It will be clear in both analyses that discourses of national identity are arranged around the construction of collective subjects (Spain, Catalonia, the Two Spains); in both analyses these subjects are assigned a certain amount of values that conform their identities; and they are even given specific spatial and temporal parameters. At times these collectivities are presented as clashing and at times the clash seems to give way to a consensus.[2]

Despite these similarities, both studies differ in their narrative approach. Chapter 2 adopts a paradigmatic narrative method, since it deals with the construction of national identities at a particular point in time: the '94 USA Football World Cup Competition. During that short period of time there was no change in the political arena and there was no change in the construction of identities. The modification in the discourses of national identity was clear in 2002, when the political turmoil had abated.

The syntagmatic approach was more suitable for chapter 3 since it deals with the development of constructions of identities throughout a short period of time in order to suit political interests. It has already been noted that after a long period of negotiation the two 'arch-enemies' Partido Popular and the Catalanists of the coalition Convergència i Unió reached an agreement that allowed the PP to gain power. At that time, on reading *La Vanguardia* daily, I realized that this Catalan newspaper was constructing the steps towards the future agreement, following a sequence of events that presented striking similarities and significant differences with the sequence of actions of a character – or 'functions' – established by the Russian formalist Vladimir Propp in his *Morphology of the Folktale*.

A foretaste of such an ideological construction will clarify this point: at an early stage after the elections, the Catalanists and Catalonia were presented as the victims of the PP, generally regarded as part of Eternal Spain – the conservative backward-looking part of Spanish society. At that point, for CiU, any kind of pact with the PP was either frowned upon or regarded as difficult to realize. Later on, when the pact became more attractive for the Catalanists, *La Vanguardia* would start to emphasize the supposed heroic role of the Catalanists and Catalonia as saviours of Spain (not new in Spanish politics, as will be seen), and to prepare the readership for the granting to the PP of the necessary 'magical agent' (the 16 parliamentary seats that CiU obtained in the elections) to sort out the situation. At the start, the PP was constructed as a 'villain' but later became a 'hero'. This passage from 'villain' to 'hero' was essential for the justification of the pact and it took the form of a 'test' or a very difficult 'ordeal' set by the Catalanists in which the PP supposedly proved their adequacy and ability to be in power.

The textual analysis of headlines, features but mainly opinion columns, shows how this particular construction of the sequence of events was as an attempt to justify a pact which was largely unacceptable to the grassroots of the Catalanist movement. It was also an attempt to make acceptable a discourse that had been rejected beforehand. The sequence implied a change in the conception of Spanish identity. As will be seen, the myths of Catalan identity remained unchanged[3].

The book will close with a general conclusion that will occupy the whole of chapter 4.

Elements of Identity

Before proceeding any further it is worth dwelling upon the elements of identity relevant in Spain and particularly relevant for this study. In Spain, the construction of national identity in terms of ethnicity, understood as race, has been ruled out just as in most of the European countries (Keating, 1988: 16), despite occasional claims of blood group distinction coming from Basque nationalists. There has been some use of racial concepts in the definition of Spanish identity (in images such as *la raza* (race), *la casta* (pedigree) but these are almost all restricted to a particular type of sport rhetoric, as will be seen in chapter 2.

Language is also a salient element of national identity in Spain – particularly in bilingual regions such as the Basque Country, Catalonia and Galicia, but also in the rest of the country as a whole. Social Identity Theory has shown that language is one of the most important dimensions of group identity and, in Spain, languages (both Castilian and the regional languages) have been used as the 'essential symbol' (Fishman, 1989: 32), 'as the medium to nationalism' (*ibid*: 270), as a weapon for legitimation and 'as an instrument of power' (*ibid*: 272). Despite the salience of language, in neither of the analyses does the controversy over the linguistic normalization of Catalan appear as a political debate. However, the strong connection between the Catalan language and Catalan identity and the implications of the use of either language in Catalonia are key in the construction of national character. In chapter 2, I will analyse a text from the Catalanist daily *Avui* written in Catalan in which the use of a number of expressions in Castilian Spanish trigger the construction of two differentiated collective identities: the Catalan and the Spanish ones.

Notwithstanding the importance of language, the elements of identity I will concentrate on are the set of values related to national or (sub-national) groups. The framework of common values supposedly constituting collective identities has a strong ideological force insofar as they are aimed at maintaining or transforming a particular relation of power within the group and in relation to other groups. An example of this point is the myth of the 'Catalan Oasis' – an expressive single image that includes a whole configuration of values related to the 'tranquil periphery' that, according to Catalan nationalism, Catalonia is. However, as Rivière points out, the image of this oasis is just a strategy with a double aim: firstly, to make believe that 'nothing happens, that in Catalonia everything is good understanding and unity' (1996: 186); and, secondly, to continue insisting on 'being different from Madrid' (*ibid*) – Madrid being commonly regarded in Barcelona as a rough place where agreements are not possible, a place full of politicians at loggerheads with each other. This book shows that in the Spanish political universe there is a certain range of values such as conviviality, good understanding, democracy, modernity, Europeanism, and civilization that are self-attributed to one's own group or negated to other groups in order to, respectively, legitimize and de-legitimize their claims.

---

[1] For a comprehensive pan-European investigation on the relationship between national identities, politics, culture and the media, see Blain *et al.* (1993).

[2] The universality of narratives has been made evident by other authors - this is indeed one of the achievements of Structuralism, and Narratology in particular to which this book owes so much. The work of the French semiotician Greimas highlights the value of narrative theory when applied to not only literary and mythical tales, but also to ethnological, psychological, sociological and scientific discourses. French philosopher Jean-François Lyotard also observes that modern science, as opposed to postmodern science, 'legitimates the rules of its own game' by means of narratives, by 'making an explicit appeal to some grand narrative, such as the dialectics of the Spirit, the hermeneutics of meaning, the emancipation of the rational or working subject, or the creation of wealth' (Lyotard, 1984: xxiii).

Within the field of mass media studies, the *Journal of Narrative and Life History* has shown in many of its articles how the mass media convey the values and attitudes that shape society in the form of stories and myths. Also within the field of media analysis, John Fiske has observed the ubiquitous form of narrative in drama, news, documentaries, sport and quiz shows and videos (Fiske, 1987: 128-129).

[3] It should be pointed out that the need for a change in the Spanish identity forms one of the premises of Catalanism. As the argument goes, it is not the identity of Catalonia that needs to be changed, but Spain's: Catalonia is generally presented by Catalanism as having a well-defined personality (which, of course, does not mean that it does not need to be promoted), whereas Spain is thrown into a potential dynamics of change; or as Ramón Pi points out, '*what Catalan nationalism debates is not what should be understood as Catalonia, but what should be understood as Spain*' (Pi and Pujol, 1996: 34, his italics).

CHAPTER 1

FOUR DISCOURSES OF SPAIN AND CATALONIA

1. Introduction

I have distinguished the four discourses regarding whether they have the whole of the state or the (Catalan) periphery as their point of reference. I have categorized the Catalan discourses as 'differential and 'disjunctive', and the all-Spanish as 'conservative unitarian' and 'liberal regenerationist'. This categorization does not have a clear-cut territorial base, since there are ideological groups that belong economically and culturally to the periphery but share the values of the centre. There are also groups whose political focus is the state as a whole, but provide a policy for the accommodation of peripheral ideology. And furthermore, groups which, although having the region as their main field of action and object of their policies, entertain ideals for collaboration in the state and even its transformation and improvement. Furthermore, these positions may vary depending on the political circumstances.

2. Two Catalanist Discourses

Following Fernández *et al.*, Catalanist conceptions of the Spanish State are based on the following axiom: 'Spain is not a nation. National unity was a reality historically imposed by the Absolutist Monarchy and has been maintained all along by the different political regimes of contemporary Spain' (Fernández *et al.*, 1983: 27). The political interpretations of this axiom have given rise to two main variants of Catalan nationalism (independence vs. devolved powers). They, in turn, have generated two types of discourse, called here 'differential' and 'disjunctive'. The idea behind this sub-categorization is the particular conception of the Spanish State and the relationship of Catalonia with it.

The differential discourse is a heterogeneous category that includes different readings that go from the least radical autonomist, to the conception of Spain as a federal State or a 'confederation of National States' (Fernández *et al.*, 1983: 29). These theories do not deny the legitimacy of the Spanish State but emphasize the idea that the State is a problematic administrative structure formed by 'different century-long national realities which are prior to the State ... which have been artificially grouped together and integrated in a centralist project by authoritarian means' (*ibid*). This theory is more concerned with home rule within a multinational state than with full independence.

The governing thesis of the disjunctive discourse is that Spain and Catalonia are two incompatible realities and that the only possible solution to the conflict is independence. Historically, this is the Catalanist trend that has had fewest adherents and least opportunities to implement its policies.

Differential Catalanism

Right Wing

Up until the mid-1920s Catalanism was primarily a middle-class conservative movement which, as Hobsbawm points out, 'belonged primarily to the local middle classes, to small-town provincial notables and to intellectuals' (1990: 146). Conservative Catalanism carried out a policy of cooperation with Central Government, as exemplified in the political action of the Lliga Regionalista, founded by Prat de la Riba in 1901. The Lliga had an ambitious project both for Catalonia and for the whole of the Spanish State – nothing less than its reform under the hegemony of the bloc formed by the bourgeoisie in Catalonia. This double Spanish–Catalan preoccupation was reflected in the manifesto 'per Catalunya i l'Espanya Gran' ('for Catalonia and a Greater Spain') written in 1916 by Prat de la Riba himself and signed by a series of Catalanist politicians.

Ever since the beginning of the century and right up to the outbreak of the Civil War in 1936, the increasing strength of Catalanism in Spanish politics displayed a moderate attitude that combined demands for more regional powers with an interest in and cooperation with central government. That was the case in the collaboration – at the beginning of the century – between Cambó (in Catalonia) and Antonio Maura (in central government) that gained Cambó the accusation of defection and betrayal. The ultimate sign of the half-way house (at times contradictory) attitude of the Lliga towards Central government was its support for the military *coup d'état* of Primo de Rivera in 1921 in the belief that 'while reestablishing order and authority, he would adopt a sympathetic attitude to Catalanism' (Keating, 1988: 99), which would be proved wrong.

Even today the proposals of political Catalanism for the whole of the State are clearly based on active intervention in the affairs of Spain. As the President of the Catalan Generalitat and leader of CiU, Jordi Pujol, observes (from the centre–right Catalanist perspective):

> the two main pillars of political Catalanism ... have been, on the one hand, and as something absolutely paramount, the national assertion of Catalonia ... But another great pillar of this political Catalanism, at least in a very important part, has been the attempt to be effectively present in Spanish politics. With the objective, on the one hand, of giving Spain a structure that allows Catalonia to fit in ... And on the other, to attempt (with a whole series of Spanish regenerationist programmes we have put forward) ... a modernization of the State, a degree of modernization of Spain (Pi and Pujol, 1996: 224).

Pujol further claims that this participation in State politics is driven by an 'ideal of grandeur' (*ibid*: 230) in the same way as Prat de la Riba and Cambó fought for a 'Catalonia and a Greater Spain'. These ambitious plans for the whole of Spain, this self-assigned role of redeemer, contrasts strongly with the accusations of 'blackmail' and 'suspicious deals' that every so often Catalanists come under in the rest of Spain and which turn them into the 'villains' of the State.

Left Wing

Until the second decade of the 20th century, the 'anarchist working class, both Catalan and migrant, remained suspicious of nationalism on class grounds' (Hobsbawm, 1990: 146). On that point, Keating further points out that

> [t]he cultural and religious revivals had little impact on the industrial working class, who tended to support the anarchist or socialist movements. These in turn often saw linguistic issues as divisive of the interests of native Catalan and immigrant workers. Catalan speaking was nevertheless widespread among the native and some of the immigrant working class and ... was to provide a basis for the nationalism of the left which emerged in the twentieth century (1988: 70).

It must be noted, however, that as early as 1848 the first federalism started to take shape as a reaction both to the centralist policies of the government and to hegemonic nationalism which was bourgeois and separated from the masses. One of the main ideologue of federalism was Pi i Margall (1824–1901), a strong defender of the structuring of Spain into regions on an equal footing. These federalist theories proposed a bottom-up construction of the State, which implied a rejection of an administrative structure imposed from the centre and a total respect for the differences amongst the regions. Pi i Margall's concern was not only the interests of Catalonia but also of the rest of Spain, while other federalist proposals such as Valenti Almirall's were more concerned with 'a solution for Catalonia' (González Antón, 1997: 480).

Pi i Margall's federalism was strongly linked to the concerns of the working class, which made it unpopular with the Catalan ruling classes, who advocated decentralization of the State but in an orderly fashion. In general, it can be said that for the working classes the regional question was not one of its priorities and it would not be until the beginning of the 20th century that Catalanism 'started to finally leave behind the indubitably reactionary connotations of the previous decades … and slowly gain wider social support' (*ibid*: 544)[1].

PSC (Partit dels Socialistes de Catalunya), the Catalan Socialist party with strong links to the PSOE and headed by Pasqual Maragall, could be regarded as the heirs of this left-wing moderate political Catalanism. CiU follows the tradition of conservative Catalanists.

What are the differences between CiU and PSC? Apart from the ideological differences within the political spectrum, these two groups differ from each other regarding the political relationship between Catalonia and the rest of Spain. According to regular columnist of *El País*, Santos Juliá, Jordi Pujol's strategy is based on:

a principle that Catalan nationalism has cultivated since Cambó: to conquer all power in Catalonia in order to be strong in Madrid. And although, unlike Cambó, Pujol has never felt tempted to exert his influence in Madrid by being part of the Governments of the State ... he has managed to have power in Madrid, especially after 1993, when absolute majorities came to an end (*El País*, 12 September 1999).

The stance of the Catalan Socialists (of Partit dels Socialistes de Catalunya, PSC–PSOE) on the Catalonia–Spain relationship is based on the recasting of such a relationship 'on a federal basis, which means a Catalonia open to dialogue with the Basque Country, but also with Andalucía or Aragón, asserting the differences but without belittling the common inheritance' (*ibid*).

The Disjunctive Discourse

This discourse gathered momentum after the First World War at the time when wide sectors of Catalan society were demanding a home-rule deal. However, (as noted above) when faced with the threat of class struggle in the period 1917–1923, the Catalan elite and middle classes withdrew from these demands for devolution and ended up supporting the dictator Primo de Rivera who crushed the working-class protests *manu militari*. Against that background the Catalanist movement of the left started to gather momentum; and if, beforehand, the compromising attitude of bourgeois Catalanism represented by Francesc Cambó prevailed, a more radical left-wing Catalanism led by Francesc Macià and his Esquerra Republicana de Catalunya developed with the aspiration of turning Catalonia into an independent Republic within a Spanish Federal State. This tendency dominated politics in Catalonia from 1931 up to the Civil War.

Two days after the victory of the left wing in the 1931 local elections (after which the Second Spanish Republic was proclaimed) the Catalan Republic of the Iberian Federation was declared, although three days later it was mellowed down to the *Generalitat de Catalunya*, based on the idea of 'self-determination' and the restoration of the unity of Catalonia. A white paper for a devolved parliament was drafted and overwhelmingly approved in a referendum – but criticized out of hand by the Right and Centre because it meant a sundering of the fatherland. The further radicalization of the political pre-war situation led the president of the Catalan Generalitat, Lluís Companys, to declare the establishment of the Catalan State of the Spanish Federal Republic. The heirs to this political movement are the left-wing Catalan nationalist party Esquerra Republicana de Catalunya which aimed at full independence beyond federalism – although nowadays the aspirations of this party vary from independence down to a co-federation with the rest of the Spanish state.

3. Two All-Spanish Discourses

The categorization of the all-Spanish discourses has been carried out along the well-established and almost mythical cleavage of Spanish society – the Two Spains, represented by two groups: the liberal regenerationists and the unitarian conservatives. At the risk of simplification, these two main discourses of Spanish national identity correspond with the centre–right conservatives and the (centre)–left-wing liberals, respectively. These two ideological trends have generated two types of verbal–ideological systems, called here the 'liberal regenerationist discourse' and the 'unitarian conservative discourse'.

The Liberal Regenerationist Discourse

The formulation of liberal regenerationist ideology took place in the last quarter of the 19th century with a new generation of intellectuals 'with concerns about the nation' (Fox, 1997: 56). This group of liberal intellectuals argued that the cause of the decline of Spain was attributable to the failure of the Restoration to modernize. The Restoration began in 1876 with the reign of Alfonso XII and provided a certain political stability based on the existence and alternation in power of two main parties: the conservatives (related to the landowning and Court aristocracy) and the liberals (representatives of the liberal professionals, traders, industrialists and middle classes). The reformists attacked the system for its inefficiency, corruption, clientelism, strong centralism, militarism, its support for the unproductive landowning aristocracy and its refusal to consider any new innovative ideas coming from the rest of Europe (García de Cortázar and González, 1994: 49) – all regarded as the causes of the backwardness of the country. The loss of the last colonies of the Spanish Empire in 1898, when Cuba, Puerto Rico and the Philippines gained independence through war with the military support of the USA, galvanized the regenerationist movement.

This movement included the writers and philosophers Ortega y Gasset, Unamuno and Costa. These authors constituted a very heterogeneous and contradictory group. Even at a personal level some of the members of this liberal regenerationist generation adopted an ambivalent attitude towards 'Spanish identity' or the means to modernize the country. In fact they did not even belong to the same generation, with Unamuno as a member of the 1898 generation and Ortega y Gasset, a member of the 1914 one. But, despite contradictions, Europeanism, positivism and respect towards the differences within the Spanish State (albeit defending the existence of a Spanish nation) are the most characteristic and lasting features of this group. As García de Cortázar and González point out, one of its most salient features was its rejection of what had been previously established as *lo español* (the essentially Spanish). This rejection was based on the unsettled concept of identity encapsulated in the motto 'the Genius of nations does not exist', which means that for them, *lo español* was only the official national identity constructed by the establishment, and could be changed. For this generation, the way to transform the national character of Spain and to tackle 'el problema de España' (that is, its backwardness) was the study and application of science and technology in economic and social life (Fox, 1997: 56), the introduction of universal education and opening out to the rest of Europe. Indeed, the regenerationists turned the European ideal into a 'programme' (Morón Arroyo, 1996: 27). Europe became a kind of transcendental category with a series of associated values (still relevant in Spanish society), to wit: philosophy, science, technology and education (Morón Arroyo, 1996: 37–51). This positivist attitude is summed up in a well-known sentence by Ortega y Gasset: 'Europe equals science; the rest is common to the rest of the planet' (Ortega y Gasset, 1946: 102).

As far as the configuration of the Spanish State, despite their general support for devolved powers, the Spanish progressive liberals were driven by a 'rationalist and uniform' conception of the state (Keating, 1988: 100), especially when confronted with the 'mystic/romantic conception of the Catalan and Basque nationalist right or the demands for self-determination voiced by the separatist left' (*ibid*). However, the all-Spanish liberal movement, faced with the danger or threat of separatism coming from peripheral nationalism, would opt to integrate rather than destroy them. Thus, the idea of the existence and the defence of a Spanish nation would not be regarded as contradictory with federalism. Following the ideas of these liberal generations, home rule was implemented during the short-lived Second Republic, and it is the model in which the present State of the Autonomies is based.

The Unitarian Conservative Discourse

From the years of the loss of the last colonies, the famous 1898 *Disaster*, centralist conservatives rejected any granting of devolved powers to the regions on the claim that giving in to the demands of the autonomists in the Colonies had paved the way towards the war and their eventual loss. This position was strong among the military, particularly after the taste of defeat brought about by the negative outcome of the war. It opened up a line of thought still present that can be summed by the following axiom: 'Only Spain is the nation. As a consequence, only Spain can develop or deploy as a unique and unified nation' (Fernández *et al.*, 1983: 24).

The situation of crisis, suspicion and fear for the unity of the country triggered by the *Desastre del '98* led to the strengthening of 'a monolithic conception of national identity constructed on a supposedly archetypal Castilian character' (Balfour, 1996: 30). The Castile of the Christian Reconquest would become the model for a new Spain. This conception of the Hispanic character was linked to the idea of Spanishness held by the Restoration system and its promotion of the imperial character of Spain with its 'universalistic mission ... to bring spirituality to an increasingly materialistic world' (*ibid*), the latter being represented by the Anglo-Saxon tradition. But not all Conservatives were complicit with the Restoration system. For an important section of reactionary Spain the incompetent political system was to blame for the loss of the Colonies. The army was the core of a new generation of right-wing regenerationists with their 'mystique of saviours of the country' (García de Cortázar and González, 1994: 545), their strong jingoism, anti-democratic ideology and loathing of Catalan particularism and its threat to the unity of the Spanish fatherland. This trend sought to modernize the nation through an authoritarian state, which would bolster the economy and would allow Spain go back to its imperial past, now with the focus on expansion into Africa.

That would be the project of the dictator Miguel Primo de Rivera, who took over in 1921 and remained in power until January 1930. Despite his initial moderation in all aspects of politics, Primo de Rivera's regime gradually became more conservative in its overall political outlook. As far as the internal structure of the State is concerned, he developed an increasing obsession with the Catalan 'threat' moving, as a result, to abolish the *Mancomunitat Catalana* (the Catalan Regional Government established in March 1914, whose doctrine was based on the so-called *Bases de Manresa* (1882) – a document that advocated the federalization of Spain).

The dictator set out to create a common national (Spanish) project which would be continued by the Franco regime. In fact, the Falange, the nationalistic organization based on Italian fascism and founded by José Antonio Primo de Rivera in 1933, provided 'volunteer companies for the Francoist rising' and, although the Falange was later marginalized by Franco, Francoism adopted not only its slogan *Spain One, Great and Free*, but also its nationalistic and authoritarian rhetoric and its symbols: the yoke and the arrows. The verbal–ideological system of Francoism deserves special attention since it enjoyed the privileged position of being the only one with official presence in the media and the education system for nearly forty years (1939–1975) – thus gaining for itself a hegemonic position.

Spain, One, Great and Free

The military led by Franco were part of an extreme brand of Spanish State nationalism which had set itself the task of freeing the country from the risk of communism, socialism, freemasonry, liberalism and disintegration (Preston, 1991: 5), all of which seemed to be part of the same ideological field. The central motto of the regime *Spain One, Great and Free* – encapsulated the centralist conception of the State. As Rodgers observes, the Francoists 'appealed to an inchoate nationalist sentiment, associated with a unitary view of the Spanish state, identified with the imperial past, and especially with the figures of the *Reyes Católicos*' (Rodgers, 1994: 53) which provided the victors with a legitimating narrative of the history of the unity of the country and also attempted to 'forge a sense of historical destiny' (*ibid*).

The idea of Spain as a 'historic unity' meant the complete elimination of devolved powers given to the regions during the Second Republic. Culturally, Franco's regime imposed on the country an official version of Spain and Spanishness based on uniformity and homogeneity, seeking to root out all traces of cultural and ideological differences. Furthermore, the 'nation' – the core of all values in the Francoist new order – was constructed as having a finality: it became 'a single, universal destiny' (*unidad de destino en lo universal*), projected as the antithesis of change (Graham, 1996: 237). The legitimizing discourse of the coup and of the whole regime promoted this idea of permanence and uniformity by constant reference to two closely related elements regarded as 'essential' to the character of Spain: her imperial glory, and her universal religious role. Franco and all the rebel commanders were part of the traditionalist and patriotic trend that identified Catholicism with the being of Spain; hence the war was turned into a religious battle and with the establishment of the dictatorship the model of national identity was based on the Reconquest, the glorification of the crusades against the Moors, and the mythologizing of the glorious centuries of the Spanish Empire (fifteenth, sixteenth, and seventeenth centuries) (Graham and Sánchez, 1996: 407); and, furthermore, the country was endowed with the responsibility of guaranteeing the continuity of the Christian values of the West (García de Cortázar and González, 1994: 590).

The Two Spains

The glorification of the imperial centuries with their 'militant and intolerant Catholicism, meant the functional resurrection of its Manichean moral categories of the two Spains' (Graham, 1996: 237). The Francoist rebellion was partly interpreted as a religious crusade, as a result of which the cleavage of the Two Spains would take on a religious perspective constituted along the dichotomy of 'the Catholic fatherland, the real Spain' versus the demonized 'Anti-Spain of Republican laicism' (García de Cortázar and González, 1994: 594), the latter being regarded as alien to the true nation. The Two Spains divide was also drawn along political lines. As Rodgers points out: '[D]emocracy had to be presented not only as a recipe for disorder but also as unauthentic, a foreign importation introduced by stealth, and its proponents denounced as traitors to their historic identity as Spaniards' (Rodgers, 1994: 54).

The cleavage between the Two Spains, a real and legitimate one and a bogus foreign-influenced one, as observed by Rodgers, was not a feature particular to the right-wing insurgents:

> both sides sought to lay claim to national authenticity by using similar rhetoric about "defending the integrity of Spain". Both republicans and insurgents regarded their adversaries as fighting, not so much for an alternative vision of Spain as against Spain. Just as the insurgents and their apologists continually alleged that the Republican government would never have come into being if it had not been for the secret machinations of Moscow, so also republicans could claim that to defend the Republic was to defend Spain against foreign dictators (Rodgers, 1994: 55).

As will be seen in chapters 2 and 3, this representation of a divided Spain is still used as a political instrument.

Spain is different

Due to the international economic embargo and political isolation imposed on the new regime, the concept of *autarquía* (autarky) came to the forefront of Spanish politics at the end of the war. Making a virtue out of necessity, Francoist Spain remained 'proudly alone' (García de Cortázar and González, 1994: 595), following the entrenched Conservative Spanish tradition of detachment in relation to the rest of the European continent. This went as far as turning down the economic help of the Marshall Plan for the recovery of European economies 'with grotesque political pride' (*ibid*: 603), resulting in the aid being delayed. After the establishment of the Common Market in 1957 Spain became definitively isolated from the rest of Europe (*ibid*: 604). Although the official attitude of the regime vis-à-vis the new European association was 'public disdain' (*ibid*: 616), there was a 'private interest' (*ibid*) in many sections of Spanish society.

Spain's international isolation and detachment was encapsulated in the slogan 'Spain is different'. As a political slogan it served to unify the nation by projecting difference outside its borders, reinforcing the idea of Spanish national identity as other than European, liberal democratic and decadent, and superior to it (Graham and Labanyi, 1996: 407). Europe was also used for defining internal otherness, the enemy within, the *Anti-España* which was 'necessarily equated with foreign influence' (*ibid*: 397)[2].

This proud isolationism would become unsustainable with the economic boom of the 1950s and 1960s, a period in which 'economic development came to Spain despite Franco's economic planners rather than because of them' (Longhurst, 2000: 18). From then onwards it would be increasingly difficult to maintain Spain for much longer in difference as the basis for a national identity. And despite the official contempt towards anything foreign, the new linking of Spain to the rest of the more advanced Western economies would strengthen the idea that Europe would be, sooner or later, the destiny of the Spaniards. The opposition entertained an idea of Europe as a symbol of democracy and progress. As will be seen, the self-attribution and denial to political rivals of the value of 'Europeanism' is still a paramount feature of the Spanish political universe.

This imposition of a unitary vision of Spain which was proudly isolated and folkloric, and the attempt to deny heterogeneity, was strongly rejected by the opposition, which ended up deeming anything Spanish as tantamount to tastelessness and worthlessness, encapsulated in the term *españolada* (a clichéd and stereotypical image of Spain). In the periphery (especially in those regions with their own strong nationalist movements), country and political system were made synonymous, i.e. Spain *was* Francoism; and, conversely, 'if Francoism monopolized Spanish national sentiment, Anti-Francoism, as a reaction, joined separatism or became sympathetic to it' (García de Cortázar and González, 1994: 590). In this period the position of Catalan nationalism strengthened through the alliance between nationalism and the ideals of the democratic opposition 'of both the right and the left, of natives and immigrants' which led to the idea that 'the fight for liberty … would entail the defense of the right of self-government and respect for the individual personality of each region' (González Antón, 1997: 620).

4. After Franco – A Renewed Clash of Discourses

Contrary to what was widely expected, after Franco's death in 1975 the debate and tension about the identity problem gathered new momentum with the development of the so-called reformation of the State through the 1978 democratic Constitution. The new democratic period did not and has not succeeded in bringing it to a conclusion. Once the Franco regime had drawn to a close, the expected consequence would have been not only that Spanishness would regain its prestige, but, more importantly, that Spanish unity would gain strength. The existence of a common enemy had clustered together the bulk of the opposition to Franco providing a well-defined outline of the culture of the resistance. Although one of the underlying ideals of the transition to democracy was that the century-old divisions between the centre and the periphery and between the two Spains would come to an end, with the whole of the country uniting behind one democratic objective, after the death of the dictator, a plurality of viewpoints re-emerged.

The new democracy had strong misgivings to dispel, since the political transition was not carried out under the aegis of complete change – a characteristic which made it liable to delegitimation. The spirit which prevailed was that of *ruptura pactada*, a negotiated break with the past. Therefore, although the death of Franco on 20 November 1975 is a crucial turning point in the history of Spain, the scope of the subsequent transformation of Spanish society and the political system is still open to different interpretations.

In the dominant interpretation of the new democracy, after the death of Franco, Spain makes a U-turn, and moves out of what is widely known as the 'long Francoist night' (*La larga noche franquista*). In the narrative accounts of the period, the idea of a 'point of no return' is frequently conveyed by means of images of death and rebirth of Spain; and through metaphors of Spain awakening from a period of 'boredom'; of becoming European and vibrant and finally boarding the train of history. Spanish new democracy is also celebrated by dominant and official version of history for the successful and peaceful changes it has undergone in such a short period of time. Special praise is commonly given to the tolerance Spain has displayed in the acceptance of its cultural and political variety in the form of its new semi-federal administrative structure. In this version of events, little by little, the new establishment and its institutions have gained stability and maturity after shaking off all the signs of 'democratic deficit' – including the Monarchy and the King Juan Carlos I, re-instated by Franco as the heir to his regime.

It is difficult not to acknowledge the fast and deep transformation of Spanish society after the death of Franco. However, non-official interpretations of events (mainly by radical peripheral nationalisms and Republicans) still entertain the idea that the new regime is a continuation of the old and, therefore, illegitimate. More moderate peripheral interpretations produce a picture of a transformed Spain but still politically bogged down in the past, since, at the end of the day, the Monarchy headed by King Juan Carlos I, was reinstalled by Franco himself[3].

A point that illustrates this controversy revolves around the European pedigree of Spanish society. On this matter, peripheral nationalists tend to harp on the idea that Spain's European and democratic spirit is dubious. However, it should be remembered that the new democratic system had, as one of its major objectives, to bring the century-long isolation of the country to an end. And this was the aim of all the main political parties. As García de Cortázar and González point out, with the Governments of Unión de Centro Democrático (the first party to rule in the new democratic period), Spain 'had stopped being *different*' from Europe (1994: 640). The 1982 elections gave the PSOE a majority with a programme that included the main ideals of the liberal regenerationists: change, modernization of the country and the consolidation of its democracy, but also central to their ideology was the Europeanization of Spain. It was a political obsession which was finally implemented with the entry of Spain into the European Community in 1986. Ever since then 'Spain was to prove one of the most pro-European countries' (Lawlor and Rigby, 1998: 40), with the Socialist governments giving their 'enthusiastic backing to any move inside the Community for greater integration' including monetary union. The PSOE even changed its anti-NATO attitude in 1985 under the argument that 'if Spain wished to join the European Community it had to be part of the West's defence system' (*ibid*: 39). This pro-European stance has been taken by the PP since March 1996 and beyond.

Despite this clear evidence, the Catalanists present themselves, or the Catalonia they claim to represent, as the only heralds of the modernization of the Spanish state via the values of Europeanism, democracy and pluralism, even to the point (as will be seen in chapter 3) of denying the modernizing and democratic pedigree of the PSOE.

5. Political Background to the Period 1993–1996

1993 Elections: The PSOE – CIU Pact

After the June 1993 general elections, the Partido Socialista Obrero Español (after 11 years of absolute majorities) was, for the first time, faced with the inability to gain an overall majority. The share of parliamentary seats was as follows:

Political Party	Seats
PSOE	159
PP	141
IU	18
CiU	17
PNV	5
HB	2
Others	7

The PSOE called for the participation in central government of the centre–right Catalanists of the coalition Covergència i Unió led by Jordi Pujol, and the centre–right Basque nationalists of Partido Nacionalista Vasco (but particularly the former). In the political negotiations which ensued, questions of devolved power to the regions, of the structure and unity of Spain, and of matters of national identity (both Catalan and Spanish) came to the fore. The attacks of the Partido Popular on the PSOE's pact with the nationalists were strong from the beginning of the term. And they became even fiercer after the June 1994 European Elections, when the PP became the most voted-for party and called for an early general election. The attacks from the PP and the dailies *Abc* and *El Mundo* (supposedly helped by Izquierda Unida in a political strategy called 'the pincer' – *la pinza*) created a taut political atmosphere in which *crispación* ('tension') was the buzzword.

The supposed illegitimacy of the Socialist government was based on the numerous cases of corruption it was involved in, but the Socialists were also heavily criticized for holding on to power by supposedly giving way to Catalanist pressure and for risking the unity and survival of Spain as a nation. According to *Abc*, José María Aznar accused the Socialist leader, Felipe González, 'of having mortgaged an important part of the State in his pact with Pujol and through not having explained the contents of the agreement and the cost' (*Abc*, 8 July 1994). Álvarez Cascos, future deputy prime minister of the PP, reproached the PSOE and CiU for having reached 'unmentionable agreements that mean the dismantling of the State as the basic institution and guarantor of national unity' (*Abc*, 18 June 1994). CiU was accused of taking advantage of the situation and of abusing the precarious political situation in order to fulfil its own financial and autonomic aspirations; of being driven by a strategy of 'blackmailing' the central government; of imposing 'demands' on a government that became a 'hostage' (*Abc*, 5 July 1994) and the consenting victim of 'heavy-handed servitude' (*Abc*, 8 July 1994).

In response to these accusations of blackmail, lies and secrecy, Pujol justified the agreement with the 'corrupt' Socialist party on the grounds of a 'sense of State' since Felipe González constituted 'a guarantee of a certain stability' (*Abc*, 4 July 1994)[4]. Duran i Lleida, leader of Unió Democràtica, one of the two member-parties of the CiU coalition, explained the pact in terms of the need for political stability in a period of economic recovery and preparation for the strict conditions for the adoption of the euro (*Abc*, 19 June 1994).

The event that caused the greatest political stir of the period in the conservative press was an interview between Pedro Solbes, the then Minister of Economy, and Jordi Pujol in the Palau de la Generalitat (the Catalan Parliament building) where the State Budget was discussed. The Socialist government claimed that the reason for the meeting taking place in Barcelona and not in Madrid was the presence of the Director of the International Monetary Fund, Michel Camdessus, in the Catalan capital. However, in its editorial of 6 June 1994, *Abc* described the PSOE as a 'National Shame', and Solbes's trip to Barcelona as a 'gesture of servile submission'. Pujol, *Abc* continued in that editorial, was not only trying to 'condition, through his nationalist extortion, the course of Spanish politics' but was also attempting 'to make his rule explicit and formal ... thus humiliating the feelings of millions of Spaniards, of the Right and of the Left, with this intolerable show of arrogance' (*ibid*).

Felipe González and his Cabinet ministers were accused in the same editorial of suffering from 'bold and anti-patriotic blindness', and were held responsible for the 'the threat to national unity that the tide of anti-Catalan feelings' and the 'consenting blackmail' were causing in the rest of Spain. The editorialist asked: 'is it part of his political project to promote barriers of misunderstanding?' And finally declared: 'Jordi Pujol is the accomplice of Felipe González and seems to be willing to harm all Spaniards in exchange for extorting economic advantages, just as he has done with the Minister of the Economy, to the shame of our national dignity' (*ibid*).

This atmosphere of political tension reached alarming levels according to newspapers more akin to the Socialists. In *El País*, Haro Tecglen (a daily columnist), drew an apocalyptic picture. In discussing the insults to Jordi Pujol launched from the Madrid press, he stated:

> the capacity for insult shown by these thugs of ours is horrifying; they return to ... the 'dialectics of the fist and pistols' of 1936 and verbal terrorism ... it is true that they inflame the old Madrid–Barcelona hatred (Pujol is not innocent) ... the return to hatred, to the assault on the person, is disturbing (*El País*, 26 June 1994).

The apocalyptic tone of this article is better understood when bearing in mind that the 'dialectics of the fist and pistols' was an anti-democratic slogan of the dictator Primo de Rivera, and 1936 marked the beginning of the Civil War, which partly broke out for reasons related to the 'threat' of national fragmentation.

As will be seen in the first analysis (chapter 2), this tense political atmosphere directly affected the radicalization of discourses of national identity during the 94

Football World Cup. The agents of the centralist and conservative press (here represented by *Abc*) would construct an image of Spain as one country, with no fissures, an ideal construction with no reference to social and political fragmentation which could undermine the premise of a united Nation. Left-wing liberals (*El País*) and more radical Catalanists (*Avui*) would take advantage of the political tension to attack and delegitimize the conservative centralist discourse. Moderate Catalanism (*La Vanguardia*) would show an already historically difficult intermediate position between the centrifugal tendencies and more unitarian trends.

1996 elections: The PP – CiU Pact

The situation changed completely after the election of 3 March 1996. This time it was the Partido Popular who was unable to win an overall majority. In the whole of Spain, the share of parliamentary seats after the election was as follows:

Political Party	Seats
PP	156
PSOE	141
IU	21
CiU	16
PNV	5
HB	2
Coalición Canaria	4
BNG	2
ERC	1
Eusko Alkartasuna	1
Unió Valenciana	1

Within Catalonia the results were:

Political Party	Seats
PSOE	19
CiU	16
PP	8
ERC	1
Others	2

Faced with these results, the PP found itself forced to start negotiations with the Catalan nationalists in order to form a government, despite the political and personal attacks they had launched against CiU and its leaders during the previous legislature. However contradictory this might sound, a pact with the PP represented an invaluable opportunity for Jordi Pujol and his coalition. After three years of political collaboration with the PSOE he knew the advantages of supporting the central government, both for his party and for the Catalan bourgeoisie, whose political representative his party is. The problem for CiU then was how to convince its grassroots of the change of attitude towards the former political enemy. As will be seen in chapter 3, with the help of *La Vanguardia*, the possibility of a pact was justified as an opportunity for the transformation not only of the PP but of the whole of the Spanish State, and, even more, of Spanish collective identity.

6. After the 2000 Elections

The collaboration between the PP and CiU was successful. CiU voted in favour of the main Governmental projects with some exceptions, such as the *Ley de Extranjería*, the Immigration law. CiU maintained its support for two main reasons: for the political and economic dividends for Catalonia brought about by the pact; and due to CiU's weak position in the Catalan Parliament and its dependence on the Catalan branch of the PP. Indeed, after the 1999 elections to the Catalan Parliament, CiU sought an agreement with the PP rather than with the left-wing nationalists of Esquerra Republicana de Catalunya.

In the 2000 elections the PP obtained the first overall majority of a right-wing party (or centre–right, as they call themselves) in post-Franco Spain. In the whole of Spain, the results of the elections were as follows:

Political Party	Seats
PP	183
PSOE	125
IU	8
CiU	15
PNV	7
Coalición Canaria	4
BNG	3
ERC	1

Within Catalonia the results were:

Political Party	Seats
PSOE	17
CiU	15
PP	12
ERC	1
IU-IC	1

Despite not being in need of any other party for the formation of Government, the PP was open-minded about future collaboration with CiU and other peripheral nationalist parties such as Coalición Canaria. Again, CiU together with *La Vanguardia* had to justify a new pact with the PP – discontinuation of the fruitful collaboration with the PP could not be justified after the 2000 election; and, moreover, the situation of dependence in the Catalan Parliament had not changed. This meant that if in 1996 CiU was represented as necessary for the transformation of the PP, and even for the change of the identity of the whole of Spain, now the PP had to be represented as fully democratic, sensitive to the idea of a plural Spain and not as the heir to Francoism. This point is of crucial importance since removing Francoist suspicions from the only party of the Right in Spain necessarily meant the disappearance of the ghost of Franco from Spanish society, that is, a total transformation of Spanish identity. Of course, this also meant the (temporary, one could say) disappearance of one of the most important delegitimizing claims of Catalanism: the non-democratic or at least not truly democratic pedigree of Spanish society. This process of justification after the 2000 election will be looked into in a brief epilogue at the end of chapter 3.

By 2002, CiU had voted in favour of the most important projects carried out by Aznar's Government, some of them very controversial, including the *Plan Hidrológico Nacional* (the law that regulates the use and transfer of river waters in Spain), the new *Ley de Universidades* (the law regulating the functioning of the Spanish University system), and the budget for the previous two years.

7. Media Outlets

Here now follows a brief introduction to the most relevant features of each newspaper analysed: the all-Spanish quality papers *Abc*, *El Mundo*, and *El País*; the Catalan *Avui* (written in Catalan), and *La Vanguardia* (published in Castilian). And the sport dailies *Marca* and *As*.

Abc

Abc is a family-owned daily traditionally related to right-wing and monarchist positions and one of the few dailies to survive the transition to democracy and the death of Franco (O'Donnell, 1999: 1). Its conservative stance was clear in its continuous attacks on the PSOE governments. As seen above, its defence of centralism became furious after the pact between the Socialist and the Catalan nationalists following the 1993 General elections. Its promotion of the idea of a united Spain is 'uncompromising' (*ibid*), a position which has turned this daily into the target of strong criticism, particularly from Catalanist quarters.

Significantly, *Abc* has a section entitled 'national news', meaning 'Spanish news' despite widespread reservations (particularly in Catalonia, Basque Country and Galicia) to identify the nation with Spain. Furthermore, most words of Catalan or Basque origin are given in the Castilian language, a practice particularly promoted by the Franco regime. For instance, the Catalan parliament, known in Catalan as the *Generalitat*, is almost invariably given as the *Generalidad*. The castilianized Convergencia y Unión is preferred to Convergència i Unió. It is not infrequent to find the very Francoist-sounding Vasconia (instead of País Vasco o Euskadi) to refer to The Basque Country. The cyclist Induráin has an accent added to his Basque surname and the tennis player Arancha Sánchez is almost never 'Arantxa' – the original Basque spelling. On average, *Abc* sold 291,950 in 2000.

El Mundo

El Mundo, founded in 1980, is a 'daily newspaper published in Madrid with a national readership throughout Spain' (*ibid*: 352). As Javier Ortiz points out, in its beginnings it was a truly independent daily that was welcomed by wide sections of society since it offered a very broad, unclassifiable ideological image, including all types of opinions, from the right to the left and even giving shelter to the ideas of peripheral nationalisms (Gil-Calvo *et al.*, 2002: 119). At the beginning, this newspaper aimed at presenting itself as the 'most modern and forward-looking of all national papers' and 'to establish itself as a source of modern investigative journalism' (O'Donnell, 1999: 352). *El Mundo* has had a clear preference for 'controversial issues' (*ibid*), which sometimes makes it border on sensationalism. This tendency towards controversies, which has earned its director Pedro J. Ramírez a reputation as a 'professional scandal-monger' (Gil-Calvo *et al.*, 2002: 13), was clear in the period after 1993 and in the unmasking of political corruption in the Socialist government. That campaign, it can be argued, was not directed explicitly against the PSOE themselves because of their ideology but because they were the party in power. Since 1996 the support of the paper for Aznar's party was clear. The sales of *El Mundo* in 1995 were 307,618 copies per day[5]. In 2000, the average number of sold copies was 302,000 per day.

El País

El País, one of Spain's leading newspapers, was launched after the death of Franco and, as a result, is 'not compromised in any way by having lived through the previous repressive regime' (O'Donnell, 1999: 386). *El País* attracts readers of a modern liberal–democratic, Europeanist and centre–left conviction. *El País* is not only 'an obligatory reference point for all serious public debate within the country' but is also highly influential in setting the agenda for public debate (*ibid*).

As far as the newspaper's conception of Spain is concerned, it has 'from the outset – in keeping with its liberal stance – championed the cause of a pluralistic view of Spain as regards the autonomous communities' (*ibid*: 387). Of the general information daily newspapers *El País* had a circulation of 420,934 in 1995. The average of sold copies in 2000 was 436,302.

La Vanguardia

La Vanguardia, founded in 1881, has since its inception been a newspaper which has espoused what might generally be termed liberal–conservative views (*ibid*: 538). Though published in Barcelona and read principally in Catalonia, it has some presence beyond Catalonia. It has always been written in Castilian (even during those moments of Spanish history when publication in Catalan would have been possible) and has tended to represent those sections of Catalan society which have taken the view that their interests are best served by Catalonia's continuing inclusion within Spain as a whole. Interestingly at the time of this study, *La Vanguardia* did not have a section specifically dedicated to Catalan news and entitled accordingly. Catalan and Spanish political news are included in the section 'Política'. The relationship between *La Vanguardia* and moderate Catalanism as represented by the coalition Convergència i Unió is pointed out by the Catalan sociologist Cardús as follows: 'what the governments of Catalonia have done, going beyond their nationalist discourse, is the defence of the socio-economic interests represented by *La Vanguardia*' (Cardús, 1995: 16). Because of this Catalanist but moderate stance, for some analysts *La Vanguardia* can be regarded as a 'regional' newspaper as opposed to 'national' (Catalan) one, since it accepts the autonomic model and has no aspirations of independence. The daily circulation of the paper in 1995 was 203,026 and 191,673 in 2000.

Avui

Some very substantial distance behind the above, in terms of circulation, comes *Avui*, founded in 1976 by Premsa Catalana and with a clear nationalist conservative stance. Its general position might be described as one of broad support for Convergència i Unió (CiU). *Avui* openly supports 'increased Catalan autonomy and increased use of Catalan language' (O'Donnell, 1999: 40). The section devoted to Spanish politics was entitled 'estat' (State) in 1994, although it has now been renamed as 'política'. Despite these changes, Cardús and Tolosa state that 'only *Avui* can be conceived of as a national daily ... [where] the use of the Catalan language is a defining factor, though not the only one in its self-definition' (1998: 44). In 1994 it was the best-selling Catalan-language daily with some 37,000 daily copies sold mainly among sectors of Catalan middle and upper-middle classes (O'Donnell, 1999: 40). The average daily sales for 2000 were 30,774.

Sport Dailies: *Marca, AS*

As appeared in 1967 and was published by the same company that launched a weekly magazine of the same name during the Second Republic (1931–36). *As* is now part of Grupo Prisa, the media group to which *El País* also belongs. In 1995 the circulation of *As* was 113,559, very low compared to its most direct competitor, the sports daily *Marca*. In 2000, the average number of copies sold daily was 181,000.

Marca, published in Madrid and an obligatory reference point for supporters of Real Madrid, was founded by the pro-Franco Falangist leader Manuel Fernández Cuesta in 1938 and dominated the market until the sixties, since it was the only sports daily in Spain. Its editorial team was exclusively formed by Falangists and was therefore a stronghold of powerful fascist rhetoric[6]. *Marca* generated a particular style and lexical system (Castañón Rodríguez, 1993: 56) and, due to its long-standing solitary position in the market, its style made an impact on the way sport and football in particular are reported in the sport media. In 1984 *Marca* dissociated itself from Medios de Comunicación del Estado (state-run media group) – having transformed by then its Francoist rhetoric and outlook. In 1996 *Marca* had the highest national circulation – 475,002 copies. In 2000, the total number was 403,000. The editing group of *Marca* (Recoletos) is strongly related now to Unedisa, the publishing group to which *El Mundo* belongs.

Nowhere is the debate on national identity more coherently expressed than in the written press. On the stage offered by the Spanish dailies, the negotiation of certain constructions of Spanish and Catalan identities is performed on a daily basis. This daily struggle is partly explainable by the powerful presence of peripheral nationalisms that propose centrifugal ways of considering Spanish identity, or even reject it. This controversy assumes the proportions of media warfare in key political moments such as the period analysed in this book. In those moments the editorials of the dailies, the opinion columns and even features and news, are enlisted more than normal in the service of the ideology and interests of the paper.

For the Spanish sociologist Gil-Calvo, traditionally the Spanish press has been and still is, belligerent and biased, it has been a 'guerilla press, settled in the trenches' from where it attacks the adversary with its 'biased partisan propaganda' (Gil-Calvo *et al.*, 2002: 66). As noted above, the tone of Spanish political debate in the 1993–1996 period was very bellicose and that will be reflected in the analyses of chapters 2 and 3. But is it really the case that the Spanish press is always partisan and militant? The epilogues of both chapters 2 and 3 contradict such a sweeping statement. They refer to the 2000–2002 period, when a relatively calm political scene (particularly concerning the centre–periphery debate) prevailed due to the pacts between the PP and CiU. At that moment, the bellicose tone of the different newspapers when dealing with national identity abated. In fact, all the dailies (with the exception of *Avui*) converged towards a more or less clear rhetoric of Spanish nationalism, so frowned upon when the debate between centralists and peripheral nationalists was at its highest point. We will return to the implications of this transformation in the above-mentioned epilogues.

Apart from the ideology of the paper, another factor is crucial when undertaking the study of media representations of national identity: market requirements. In this sense, Blain *et al.* have shown that the increase in the aggressive appeals to chauvinistic sort of nationalistic sympathy in the British media can be put down (amongst other factors) to 'market utility' (*ibid*: 34). For example, the authors in part see the fairly overt recent anti-Englishness in the Scottish media as a result of market competitiveness; or put differently, as an attempt by Scottish papers to 'outscot' one another by using the anti-English feeling.

This ruling of the market can also be observed in Spain. For example, in order to maximise readership and revenues, it seems to be necessary for a specialist (and presumably 'apolitical') sports daily (like *As* or *Marca*) to treat football as commodity spectacle – which involves, among other things, dramatization, attractive use of colour, excitement, binary oppositions and the use of stereotypes. It also appears to be essential for these dailies to accept the value systems and assumptions which are not only more familiar to the readers, but also most widely legitimated – and these values include strong identification with the national team and the use of a more or less aggressive nationalistic rhetoric.

The British case, however, cannot be extrapolated to Spain due to the social, political and cultural characteristics of the country. In order to illustrate this point let's remain in the field of sports journalism. In Spain, where the 40-year Franco regime promoted the complete identification of all Spaniards with the Spanish national football team as a catalyst for the values of patriotism, the presentation of information related to the team, following the conventions of objective journalism, is not only an index of 'serious journalism' but also as a step away from Francoist and right-wing rhetoric. And vice versa: the combination of subjective points of views, direct involvement of the reader, and identification with the team in sporting reports typical of, for example, the conservative daily *Abc*, is widely interpreted by more liberal newspapers, such as *El País*, as a continuation of the kind of rhetoric established in the years of the dictatorship.

It would be naïve to think that Spanish quality newspapers are not subject to market demands – at the end of the day, they are companies trying to make a profit; but it can be rightly said that in dailies such as *El País, La Vanguardia, Avui, El Mundo* or *Abc* ideology and political stance is more of a factor than market demands. It can be argued that *Abc*'s tendency to identify with the team along the lines of the rhetoric established during the Francoist regime should be seen mainly as an index of its ideological stance and not as a market requirement. In the same vein, the atmosphere of polemic and conflict created by *Abc* with their series of attacks and accusations against Convergència i Unió during the period 1993–1996, had very little to do with an attempt to catch readers and a lot with a political intention to delegitimize the PSOE–CiU coalition in order to bring down the Socialist government.

---

[1] It should not be forgotten that at that time, the discontent of the working classes was capitalized on by Alejandro Lerroux (a strong enemy of bourgeois separatism) and not by left-wing Catalanism.

[2] Traces of the idea that the rest of the world despises Spain (and anything Spanish) were still found during coverage of the 2002 Roland Garros Tennis Championship. According to the sports editing team of *Abc*: the possibility of an all-Spanish match at the Roland Garros Championship was 'too much for our neighbours, who still fear the worst: another Spanish final'; according to the article the 'Armada' was not welcome and some top Spanish players were made to play 'in badly kept grounds' (7 June 2002). The final was indeed between the Spaniards Albert Costa and Juan Carlos Ferrero. At the press conference after the match an American journalist asked Costa what Spaniards put in their water to make them so successful at tennis. This rather innocent question was interpreted as a sign of 'bad blood' (8 June 2002), as an accusation of drug taking. That was the only example I could register (fortunately, I should say).

[3] For more information on these two conflicting interpretations of the political transformation of Spanish society after the death of Franco, see León Solís, F., 'Transition(s) to Democracy and Discourses of Memory', *International Journal of Iberian Studies*, 16: 1, 2003.

[4] As will be seen in Chapter 3, the sense of state and the 'governability of Spain' would also be two of the main arguments for the justification of the pact with the PP after the 1996 elections.

---

[5] For an interesting (albeit not complete) history of *El Mundo* since its independent beginnings to its support for Aznar, see Gil-Calvo, E., Ortiz, J., Revuelta, M. (2002), *Repensar la prensa*, Debate, Madrid.

[6] For information on the relationship between Francoism and Football, see Shaw, 1987.

CHAPTER 2

THE GAME OF THE NATION
Football and Identity

1. Introduction

The 1994 World Cup constituted a stage where the struggle for the re-construction of national identity was symbolically performed; with the background of the agreement between PSOE–CiU and the political and territorial tension spurred on by the conservative media, it became a field of contention where hegemony over a conception of the country was established: the ideological agents of conservative Spanish centralism used national team football in order to promote an idea of a single Spanish identity; more liberal agents promoted a national cleavage along the lines of the liberal–conservative divide, where the conservatives were presented as Francoist, imperialistic and jingoistic. For more radical Catalan nationalists the very same Spanish football team was used as a vehicle of nationalist expression by means of rejection of its associated political values. As will be seen in the brief epilogue at the end of this chapter, by 2002, once the political turmoil had abated, the features of and interrelationship between discourses showed some differences: while the conservative discourse of *Abc* and the Catalanist *Avui* stuck to their guns, the rest of the newspapers moved towards the patriotic rhetoric rejected in 1994 as a sign of Francoism.

2. Sport and Discourses of National Identity in Spain

The Unitarian Conservative Discourse

In his seminal book *Fútbol y Franquismo*, Shaw observes that before the Civil War (1936–1939) 'football was only politicized in its regional aspect' (Shaw, 1987: 20). However, before the Franco regime the political manipulation of sport was already a controversial issue that went beyond the regional debate. For example, the philosopher and academic Miguel de Unamuno had, in typical regenerationist–liberal fashion, already attacked the exaggerations of jingoism in sport in many of his articles in the 1920s. Despite this awareness of the political potential of football, 'the interest of the government for the game and its control over it was very weak; the clubs and the Royal Spanish Federation ... enjoyed almost complete independence from the Madrid authorities' (Shaw, 1987: 20), with the result that they kept enjoying independence and power until the Civil War (*ibid*: 38).

With Franco the situation changed completely. Even before the war had finished the sporting ethos of the Franco regime was in place and sport was being heavily used as a weapon of political action. One of the first objectives of the new regime was to eliminate the sporting rhetoric of the Second Republic which, due to its brief life (from 1931 until the breakout of the Civil War in 1936), could not implement the changes to Spanish society (which also affected sport) that its liberal ideology aspired to. For Francoist propaganda the second Republic 'became synonymous with sporting weakness and disunity' (London: 1996: 204).

The *Consejo Nacional de Deportes*, or Ministry for Sport, created in 1938, imposed a whole range of fascist symbols and rituals such as the fascist salute and the use of blue tops instead of the – until then – traditional red ones, a colour too closely identified with Communism. Other impositions included the change of names of the clubs in order to eliminate words that sounded foreign or belonged to any of the peripheral languages of Spain, or the proviso that at least two members of the board of directors of each club should be Falangists (Shaw, 1987: 82). Within the media field, the Falange, which was initially responsible for the media and propaganda policies of the new regime, regarded sport as an excellent instrument to mobilize and forge the citizens in the national spirit and the new values. As early as 1939 the president of the *Consejo Nacional de Deportes*, General Moscardó, established one of the values of Spanish sport, the implications of which are still currently controversial: its military tone. The General established that the *Consejo Nacional de Deportes* 'would be made up solely of military men so that Spanish sportsmen would be subject to military discipline', a move which gave rise to a constant relationship between sport and military endeavour (London, 1996: 204).

The values put forward by Francoist propaganda were clearly linked to the 'renewal of traditional views about Spanish history and the nature of Spanishness [that] laid stress on a universalistic mission of Spain to bring spirituality to an increasingly materialistic world' (Balfour, 1996: 30). The predominance of irrational and spiritual values over more practical considerations such as technique (promoted by the liberal discourse) were epitomized in concepts such as *furia* (fury, a concept synonymous with aggression); or charged with strong racial connotations, as in concepts such as *raza* (race) and *casta* (pedigree). As Helen Graham points out, the concept of *casta* and *casticismo* was created as a substitute for the ideology of imperialism. *Casticismo*, the same author argues, worked as an 'internalization of the Empire' the function of which was to reinforce an exclusive construction of the 'nation' (Graham, 1996: 238). This concept not only has a strong racial connotation but also a definite association with centralism as the ideal state structure, which in practice equates what is *castizo* with what is 'typically Spanish' and ultimately with what is Castilian (Graham and Labanyi, 1996: 420). Probably due to its racist overtones, this concept has almost disappeared from the sports media.

Francoist sport discourse, from its strong fascist rhetoric of the beginning to the diluted form of the last years can rightly be regarded as a foundational discourse, as the referential frame against which all other discourses are partly constructed, and around which other discourses gravitate. Examples of the promotion or rejection of the concept of *Furia* as epitome of Spanish identity can be observed in the following texts, both from the 1994 World Cup Magazine of *El País* of 16 June. The first is a quotation of the words of Luis Ramallo, MP for the Popular Party, the second, an excerpt from the introductory editorial article to the World Cup Magazine:

> The national team Coach should make use of Spanish Blood for a good performance. Spanish Fury can be an antidote to neutralize other teams' technique. Mr. Clemente, don't let it be shown [the MP probably meant don't let them think] that we have milk running through our veins, but hot blood, Spanish blood (*El País*, 16 June).

> [The Spanish team has always been subjected to] a purposeless, empty and reactionary leadership, concealed behind words as stupid as *la furia* (fury), *la garra* (grit), *el tesón* (determination), *la lucha* (fighting spirit) ... Aesthetic poverty ... clumsy football, encouraged by the cavern (*El País*, 16 June).

the 'cavern' being a metaphor for the 'primitive' and 'backward' space supposedly occupied by the Right Wing.

As will be seen in more depth in the next section, the importance of spiritual values over technique, and the experience of sport as a quasi-religious experience are at the basis of the struggle between the supporters of unitarian–conservative conceptions of Spain and the heralds of more liberal and 'peripheral' ideas of the country.

The Liberal Discourse

The origins of the liberal approach to sport have to be sought among the regenerationists of the beginning of the 20th century. Castañón Rodríguez observes that 'literature on sport appears with the '98 Generation ... [and their] anxious preoccupation for the backwardness of Spain, their search for solutions to create a modern State through the imitation of foreign technologies and ideologies, and their exaltation of a new patriotism' (Castañón Rodríguez, 1998). One of the early advocates of this need to modernize through technology and science was Miguel de Unamuno, with his characteristic indictment of Spanish obscurantism and the praise of European progress and science. He would not be the only intellectual to be interested in the relationship between sport, nationalism and patriotism, but a brief reference to his ideas will serve as an example for the whole liberal regenerationist ideology.

Castañon Rodríguez points out that Unamuno detested 'ritualistic forms of patriotism' (1998) and criticized 'the transformation of sport into a patriotic mission as opposed to its educational mission' (*ibid*). The defense of reason, culture and education versus sport nationalism is evident in *Intelectualismo y deportismo* ('Intellectualism and Sportism') (published on 21 February 1923 in the Argentinian daily *La Nación*), where he established a dividing line between 'sportism' (the mythical dimension of sport in terms of national identity) and the world of culture, to the point of talking of 'an alliance of militarism–clericalism–sportism against intellectuality' (*ibid*). According to Unamuno, this alliance promotes 'a civic education of a pre-military nature that praises chance and various non-intellectual values that hamper spiritual renovation' (*ibid*) and work against 'civilization, and end up in a violent and catastrophic commotion that makes recovery impossible' (*ibid*). It will be seen below how these preoccupations (albeit modified) are still present in Spanish society.

It was not until the restoration of democracy after Franco's death in 1975 that the general ideals of the liberals had any official recognition. In 1977, sport would become part of the Ministry of Culture. The new democratic regime, at least theoretically, promoted plurality and other social values aimed at freeing sport from particular beliefs (Castañón Rodríguez, 1993: 62), in line with more general ideals of modernization of the country, improvement of the quality of life and the uplifting of the people with a higher degree of civilization (*ibid*).

The new media context (with its privatization, regionalization and deregulation, from 1982, of the media) paved the way to the free denunciation of the political use of sport under the Franco regime (indeed, already initiated in the 60s), and a gradual decline of both Francoist sport rhetoric and of the use of typical images associated with Spanish sport and national character such as *Furia*, *Casta* and *Raza*. As Castañón Rodríguez points out, there was an attempt to wipe out 'the sports language used until then on two fronts: the proclamation of new sporting values and the satirising of the old ones' (Castañón Rodríguez, 1993: 17).

The conception of Spain as *One, Great and Free*, and its unitarian and imperialistic reflections in sport rhetoric, started to crumble in the early eighties if not in the late seventies. If in Francoist rhetoric Spanish society was perceived as forming a fundamentally homogeneous nation in which status, class, or regional divisions were superficial, now the agents of the new discourses of national identity competing for the establishment of a new conception of Spain were free to place the emphasis on 'difference'. Spanish liberals exploited the ideological divide of the Two Spains to undermine the still predominant Francoist unitarian rhetoric. In 1994 the image of Spanish society as divided into two factions and into clearly differentiated sub-national identities was used to delegitimize the then fierce conservative discourse of *Abc* and the PP and their attack on the supposedly anti-patriotic PSOE–CiU entente.

The Peripheral Discourse: The Case of Catalonia

The division between centre and periphery in Spain is particularly obvious in football, to the extent that, according to Shaw:

> the main feature of Spanish football has been the struggle between two powerful clubs [Barcelona and Real Madrid], a struggle that has been performed at three different levels: at a merely sporting level ... at a regionalist level between the two clubs that best represent Catalonia and Castile; and at a political ... level, particularly during the Franco regime, between one club regarded as right-wing and

Francoist and another considered as liberal and opposed to the regime (Shaw, 1987: 62).

During the Francoist period, Barcelona Football Club strengthened its status as a platform for the use of Catalan and as an institutional emblem, which resulted in the motto '*El Barça es mès que un club*' ('Barça is more than a club'). The club, as the Catalan writer Vázquez Montalbán points out, owes its 'meaning to the historical misfortunes of Catalonia, in everlasting real or metaphorical Civil War with the Spanish State' (Vázquez Montalbán, 1999: 5), and 'fulfils a role in the construction and deconstruction of the collective Catalan grievances' (*ibid*: 7). That situation has not changed despite efforts by club managers to eliminate any political links. In that sense, Shaw rightly points out that 'Barcelona ... is indeed the Catalan national team' (Shaw, 1987: 62), despite the fact that a large majority of its players are foreign. It can be rightly said that the Catalan club has become a totem, the depository of Catalan values. In that sense, for the President of the *Generalitat de Catalunya*, Jordi Pujol, 'Barça is one of those institutions that the country [Catalonia] has created in a natural fashion' (Pi and Pujol, 1996: 164).

And what are these values Barça is associated with? A short excerpt from an article published in *Avui* in 1994 about the then national coach Javier Clemente (originally from the Basque Country) will suffice to show these values. One important thing to note here is that the values invested in this Catalan team are the opposite of those that supposedly characterize the Spanish team. In the text the dichotomy between 'primitivism' and 'modernity' is clear; and it is worth highlighting the reference to the jingoism that the Spanish national team supposedly generates in the Spanish press. All the players mentioned here played at that time for Barcelona Football Club (none of whom is a Catalan!):

> Clemente, a Basque from head to toe, is very much to the liking of Spain. For lovers of football, however, it's a different story. Used to Koeman's geometrical passes, Laudrup's sinuosities, Stoichkov's corrosive gallop, Romario's lethal ballet, or Salinas's sense of the unexpected, his kick-and-rush tactics mean going back to football's Neanderthal age. It's obvious that a machine – even a footballing one – will fail to ignite passions, whereas race and genius, kicking and shooting to the heavens are the stuff of patriotic, adversarial, transcendental reports and broadcasts. Clemente is in the

service of a Sense of Spain with capital letters (*Avui*, 30 June).

3. Textual Analysis

3.1. Monoglot and Heteroglot Discourses

Beyond this categorization of discourses, the present analysis focuses on the mode interaction of all these discourses, and to that purpose Mikhail Bakhtin's ideas have been a fundamental source of inspiration for this analysis. In *The Discourse of the Novel* Bakhtin sets out to describe the distinctive features of the novel by centering on two concepts which are basic for my analytical purposes: dialogism and heteroglossia. Heteroglossia, in Bakhtin's own word 'is another's speech in another's language' (Bakhtin, 1981: 324). For Bakhtin:

> [A]t any given moment of its historical existence, language is heteroglot from top to bottom: it represents the co-existence of socio-ideological contradictions between the present and the past, between differing epochs and the past, between different socio-ideological groups in the present, between tendencies, schools, circles and so forth, all given a bodily form. These "languages" of heteroglossia intersect each other in a variety of ways, forming new socially typifying "languages" (*ibid*: 291).

A concept closely related to heteroglossia is dialogism, defined by the editor of Bakhtin's work as:

> the characteristic epistemological mode of a world dominated by heteroglossia. Everything means, is understood, as a part of a greater whole – there is a constant interaction between meanings, all of which have the potential of conditioning others (*ibid*: 426).

As Bakhtin notes, this dialogism does not have an 'external compositional form of dialogue' (*ibid*: 279). The mode of interrelation and competition between discourses should be seen within the framework of what has been called the 'interdiscursive space' (León Solís and O'Donnell, 1995), understood as the interface between all the discourses. In this space discourses contend for supremacy regarding the meaning of the common elements, which, in this analysis are: nation,

Spanish identity, Catalan identity, the past, the present, democracy, modernity, Europe.

Although the scope of Bakhtin's work is mainly literary, Bakhtin himself states that 'the dialogic orientation of discourse is a phenomenon that is, of course, a property of *any* discourse' (*ibid*: 279). Notwithstanding the fact that all discourses have this essential tendency, 'concrete historical human discourses ... can deviate from such inter-orientation' (*ibid*: 279) although 'only on a conditional basis and only to a certain degree' (*ibid*: 279). Therefore, any representation, any image of an object, for example, the Spanish football team, 'may be penetrated by this dialogic play of verbal intentions that meet and are interwoven in it; such an image need not stifle these forces, but on the contrary may activate and organize them' (*ibid*: 277).

Bakhtin establishes two attitudes towards this 'natural' orientation of human discourses: stifling heteroglossia within or using heteroglossia as an organizing tool. According to Bakhtin, the first tendency is typical of poetry (or rather, of a narrow conception of it), and the second of the novel (*ibid*: 277–278). This distinction can be extrapolated to other types of discourse, and without any doubt, to the subject matter of this analysis. As will be argued below, the unitarian discourse (as in the daily *Abc*) shares many features of the poetic discourse where 'the word forgets that its object has its own history of contradictory acts of verbal recognition, as well as that heteroglossia is always present in such acts of recognition' (*ibid*: 278). In that sense, it will be seen how *Abc*, in order to construct an image of an united nation, 'forgot' to acknowledge the existence of interpretations of the Spanish national team which would contradict the conception of Spain of the paper.

The agents of the other discourses (as in *El País* or *Avui*) adopted a more 'prosaic' attitude whereby 'the object reveals first of all precisely the socially heteroglot multiplicity of its names, definitions and value judgments' (*ibid*: 278). Like a prose writer, during the 1994 World Cup, all quality papers analysed except *Abc* confronted 'a multitude of routes, roads and paths that have been laid down' in the team 'by social consciousness' (*ibid*: 278). Instead of ignoring controversy and debate, these papers emphasized 'the internal contradictions' of the Spanish team. Those contradictions bore witness to 'the unfolding of social heteroglossia *surrounding* the object, the Tower-of-Babel mixing of languages that goes on around any object' (*ibid*).

3. 2. The Monoglot Discourse: the Monolithic Society

<u>The National Supporter</u>

In the 1994 championship Spain was in the same group as Germany, South Korea, and Bolivia. In the second round Spain played (and beat) Switzerland, to be finally defeated by Italy in the quarter-finals.

The use of the first-person plural possessive adjective in 'our players' and 'our team' establishes a bond between the author and the reader through the team. On 20 June 1994 *Abc* stated in its front-page headline about the coach's choice of goalkeeper: 'Zubizarreta will return to the team tomorrow'. This information was complemented in the subtitle: 'Clemente is firm in this decision and, for the good of our team, let's hope he's not mistaken'. On 7 July 1994, *Abc* celebrated the rest that the Spanish team was enjoying, three days longer than its rival Italy: 'a rest three days longer for *our team* than for the next rival' (*Abc*, my italics).

As Gastil points out in his study on political discourse, 'speakers can judiciously distribute pronouns, such as *we* and *they*, to suggest their membership or identification with different groups, such as organizations, ethnic groups or parties' (Gastil, 1992: 484). But this 'identification' with the team can go a step further: in *Abc* the reader played, together with the author, the role of actor/participant. This role corresponds to the communication situation in which the narrating voice makes itself present, or 'visible and therefore speaks more or less openly from its own point of view'. Lyons defines this kind of communicative situation as 'experiential', a term which 'is suggestive of the kind of description that might be given by someone who is personally involved in what [he/she] is describing' (1977b: 668). The audience, for its part, is a clear party in the communication process and is constructed in an active manner. That is, the reader is constructed as a supporter.

Many examples could be adduced, all along the same lines as the following two: on 21 June 1994 Fernández de Córdoba consoled himself and his readers before the match against mighty Germany by pointing out that 'the only thing we can aspire to [is] to take them by surprise...'. Just before the match against Italy at quarter-finals, where Spain was eliminated, the same columnist foresaw a glorious future for the Spanish team, referred to as 'we': 'we might reach so high that we might touch the sky' (*Abc*, 6 July 1994).

Furthermore, in their role of supporter, the author and the readers not only 'live a symbolic bionic unity with the team', but also 'cheer them on' (Verdú, 1980: 7). The day of the Spain versus Bolivia match, *Abc* encouraged Spain in the headline: 'Spain, now for Bolivia' (*Abc*, 27 June 1994); and two days later, after the victory over Bolivia, the paper exclaimed: 'And now for Switzerland' (*Abc*, 29 June 1994). The day of the final showdown against Italy, *Abc* wrote the enthusiastic headline: 'Now, Now, Now, Spain' (8 July 1994).

Four days after the elimination of Spain at the hands of Italy, the Tour de France commenced and *Abc* wrote in its editorial: 'Today the Spanish supporters, saddened by the bitter defeat of the Spanish national team in the USA World Cup, vibrate' with Indurain (12 July 1994). This highly emotional speech is one of the features of the supporter who, as Verdú points out, 'goes to the stadium to suffer' (Verdú, 1980: 25). On the day of the decisive match against Bolivia, the columnist Rafael Marichalar asked: 'and what does the man in the street think? Nobody is writing them off as defeated, but there is a certain sense of fear in the air' (*Abc*, 27 June 1994). This emotional engagement with the national team, the construction of the country as a 'sentient being' (Blain *et al.*, 1993: 80) should be seen as a politico-ideological statement. The implications of this 'football enthusiasm' will be given proper significance when the heteroglot (and non-sentimental) discourses are dealt with below.

Another main feature of sporting rhetoric in *Abc* is that the bond established between author and reader in these quotes is most the times extended to the whole of Spanish society, ignoring the fact that for many, in regions such as Catalonia and the Basque Country, the Spanish team is a controversial institution. Despite this fact, the day of the match against Germany *Abc* wrote on its front page: 'millions of Spaniards will again close ranks around the national team' (21 June 1994). Before the match against Bolivia which would decide whether Spain would qualify for the second round, *Abc* offered the following front-page headline: 'the whole of Spain will be following the match' (27 June 1994).

The emotion of this united country and the performance of the team often acquired a national significance. The qualification of the noun 'team' by the adjective 'national' in 'the national team' is criss-crossed with heavy political implications: as seen in chapter 1, what constitutes the nation for Catalans (whether it is Spain or Catalonia or both) is part of a long-standing debate. However, for *Abc* the matter is quite clear. On 2 July 1994, the day in which Conchita Martínez was playing the final in Wimbledon and Spain was playing Switzerland, *Abc* wrote in its headlines: 'Two great events where our star sporting representatives will have the whole of the nation on tenterhooks' (*Abc*, 2 July 1994). In an article epically titled 'In Search of a Feat', Rafael Marichalar remembered how the victory of Spain over Denmark in Mexico 86 'caused national enthusiasm' (*Abc*, 21 June 1994). The day of the match against the Italian team, Spain and Italy were described as 'two expectant nations' (*Abc*, 7 July 1994). In these examples the acceptance of the existence of a political and sociological entity called the Spanish nation (with all its sentimental connotations) is undeniable. In opposition to the frequent use of the attribute 'national' in conservative papers (and sports dailies such as *Marca* and *As*), the peripheral nationalist papers opted for the use of expressions such as 'the state team' (as the Basque nationalist paper *Deia* put it, on June 22, 1994), which refer to a Spain understood as a mere administrative entity.

One of the most interesting features of *Abc* is that despite its preoccupation with the risk of territorial fragmentation of Spain evident in its political pages and its attacks on PSOE for their 'contra-natura' pact with CiU, nowhere in the sporting reports, opinion columns or editorials devoted to the Spanish team was the style of emotional identification with the national team and social unity ever challenged. At that particular time *Abc* appeared to adhere to the maxim that 'politics and sport don't mix' or, more prescriptively, 'politics should be kept out of sport' (Rowe, 1996: 104–105), undoubtedly because day-to-day politics referred to a reality of political, ideological and territorial segmentation that did not match up with the totemic function of the national team.

Javier Clemente: a Storm in a Teacup

In *Abc*, whatever differences of class or territory divide Spanish society, Spain is still regarded as a Nation, as a fraternal 'community ... conceived as a deep, horizontal comradeship' (Anderson, 1983: 16). This comradeship demands the negation of ideological differences and a silencing of other discourses that could jeopardize the stability of the values being defended in the sporting pages. In that sense, the unitarian discourse, in its attempt to seek 'unity in diversity' (Bakhtin, 1981: 274), ignored 'the word of the other', thus constituting a closed system dealing with nothing beyond it, no other value systems, no other points of view. As in the case of the poetic discourse 'the word does not encounter in its path toward the object the fundamental and richly varied opposition of another's word. No one hinders this word, no one argues with it' (*ibid*: 276).

Evidence of this silencing of controversy in order to seek unity in diversity was the treatment of the then coach, Javier Clemente, in *Abc*. The opposite was one of the main features of the rest of the newspapers analysed. Clemente is a self-confessed Basque nationalist, but this was not a major point. The coach's predicament was rather due to personal and professional factors. Personally he was depicted as proud and stroppy; professionally he was accused of failing to provide the team with a particular style, as he would change tactics according to the rival.

On the issue of his personality, all newspapers agreed: the sports daily *As* observed that 'pride should never lead anybody to think that they are immune to the possibility of making mistakes' (12 July 1994). The editor of the same daily, García Candau, described Javier Clemente as: 'a monomaniac ... the epitome of to each his own' (*As*, 1 July 1994). Disapproval of Clemente's personality also became a major point in *Abc*, but at no time did it hamper the fulfillment of the unifying totemic function of the national coach and it was not used to generate an image of a divided country. In that sense, M. Fernández de Córdoba remarked:

> If [victory] comes ... it will never come by way of show ... Clemente is succeeding ... in making many Spaniards happy with Spain's defeats, they would do anything to avoid seeing him showing off or looking for arguments with anyone ... He discourages rather than encourages you, he separates more than unites. Anything could be forgiven if there were a victory. Not him, but the team in spite of him (*Abc*, 21 June).

In this text, Fernández de Córdoba complains about the dysfunction of the totemic figure of the coach. However, support for the team 'in spite of him' redeems the lack of unity which Javier Clemente supposedly failed to generate, and, in fact, reinforces the image of a united country.

In the rest of the quality papers the divisions generated around Javier Clemente were beyond the personal level and were assigned clear political implications, and, what is more important here, were related to questions of national identity. In the case of *Avui*, the national identity dimension was sometimes expressed in terms of *seny*, which is a form of compromising 'common-sense' generally regarded in Catalonia as something quintessentially Catalan. The Catalan writer Margarita Rivière defines this concept as:

the exquisite contention of common sense ... a strategy involving ability, extremely basic courtesy that disconcerts would-be enemies; it's made up of moderation, of a willingness to negotiate, of rationalism, and springs from the idea that there is a need to convince the other that one is right, because all things Catalan are thoroughly thought out before they get done ... The secret of *seny* is its status as a counter figure of dogmatism, of the arbitrariness characteristic of absolute and centralized power (Rivière, 1996: 84–85).

Thus *Avui* ironizes: 'Clemente never lets you down. When he speaks ... because he always goes beyond *seny*, beyond what is predictable and goes into the field of defamatory and cutting remarks, of radicalism ... In the background of all he says there is ... a very typically Basque anti-liberal component' (*Avui*, 31 June 1994). Here *Avui* was constructing an image of Catalonia in contrast to the Basque Country. The anti-liberal Basque component refers, undoubtedly, to the radical division of Basque society into nationalists and anti-nationalists and, more importantly, to the existence of terrorist violence, regarded, one might think, as the result of the absence of the compromising spirit that the term *seny* implies. But for *Avui*, Clemente was not just Basque. As seen above, for *Avui*, ignoring the huge controversy around the coach, 'Clemente, a Basque from head to toe, is very much to the liking of Spain' (*Avui*, 30 June 1994). Just as *Abc* was excluding political controversy from sport in order to construct an image of a united Spain, *Avui* was eliminating the controversy about the coach (even ignoring his Basque nationalist credentials) in order to argue that 'Clemente is in the service of a Sense of Spain with capital letters' (*Avui*, 30 June 1994), a Spain that lacks that most Catalan of attributes: *seny*.

Clemente's professional predicament was due to his alleged lack of a sense of aesthetics and lack of a sporting style that might give an imprint or identity to the national team. Let's deal with the first element: aesthetics. As Vicent Verdú points out, aesthetics is essential in the construction of a bond between supporters and the team:

> supporters ... can barely stand their team playing badly, whether
> they win or not. Indeed, they really want to see them win, but their
> great affection for the symbol prevents them from reaching
> complete satisfaction if success is achieved in tortuous matches,
> lackluster fights and victories without glory (1980: 134).

Not surprisingly, *Abc* in its role as national supporter of the team, had this as one of its major complaints. Fernández de Córdoba, for instance, wrote in *Abc* after the match against Bolivia: 'Spain won. And I'm as happy as anyone else. As usual. And I hope they keep on winning. Shame that, in a World Cup of silk, we should provide the rough material' (*Abc*, 29 June).

For other papers the 'rough material' was more than just a sporting style and was indeed given a political dimension. In *La Vanguardia* (and other papers as will be seen below) the supposedly unsophisticated style of the team was just reminiscent of the Francoist regime: 'Clemente ... would rather sound the alarm, the urgent call to fighting spirit ... in defence of the colours of the fatherland. This team is somewhat antique ... Clemente is for restoring the *furia* that made us different' wrote Enric Bañeres (4 July 1994).

This re-politization of Clemente's style was also present in the interpretation of his supposed lack of a style representative of Spanish Football. The Catalan philosopher and columnist of *La Vanguardia* Josep Ramoneda, interpreted the lack of a particular style in Clemente's team along the lines of the state/nation divide:

> Spain, no matter how hard some try to restore the Francoist
> rhetoric, lacks in identity ... it is a reflection of a country that
> has separated what belongs to the state from what belongs to
> feelings. The team is a superstructure; the clubs channel
> [Catalan/Basque] national feelings. Some teams are more than
> a club, Spain is less than a national side (3 July 1994).

Contrary to the display of division within Spain, *Abc* shrouded the team in a patriotic and deproblematized atmosphere that veiled ideological and territorial conflict, which, however, populated the political pages of the daily, mainly focused on the supposedly unnatural pact between Socialists and Catalanists. Even in the opinion columns outside the sport section there was a refusal to politicize the team.

Following the elimination of the team against Italy, Jaime Campmany (an *Abc* columnist famous for his Francoist past), jokingly wrote:

> Clemente has divided Spain with a new line, and now we have the sunny Spain and the shadowy Spain, the wet one and the dry one, the red and the blue, the one of the central plateau and the one of the coasts, and now the one that praises Clemente and the one that crucifies Clemente (*Abc*, 12 July).

Campmany, in his typical parodic tone, played down the politico-ideological divide of the Two Spains by relating it to other geographical, climatic and ad hoc divisions – 'the red and the blue' referring to the Civil War division between the Popular-Front left-wing and the right-wing Francoist supporters, respectively. For Campmany, the polemic generated around Clemente might reflect two points of view, there might not be general agreement around the national symbol, but, as in the case of poetic discourse, this polemic is a joke of no importance, and it is made to remain

> within the boundaries of a single hermetic and unitary language system, without any underlying fundamental socio-linguistic orchestration ... The internal bifurcation (double-voicing) of discourse, sufficient to a single and unitary language and to a consistently monologic style ... is merely a game, a tempest in a teapot (Bakhtin, 1981: 325).

3.3. Heteroglot Discourses

Introduction

In this section I will look into the heteroglot discourses (those of *El País, Avui, El Mundo* and *La Vanguardia*) for which the polemics and divisions generated around the team and the coach were not just 'storms in a teacup' but real reflections of socio-political divides. Those discourses presented two main features relevant for this analysis (and which Bakhtin associates with the novel):

a) They placed the national team in a historical dimension. The historical perspective (as opposed to the 'experiential perspective' adopted by *Abc*) goes hand in hand with the spectator position adopted by the speaker, whose voice is 'above' the events, issues and persons she/he describes. Lyons describes this enunciative situation as 'historical', a term 'intended to suggest the narration of events, ordered in terms of successivity and presented dispassionately with the minimum of subjective involvement' (Lyons, 1977b: 668). In this type of communicative situation there is no direct addressing of the reader and there is no encouragement for his/her participation. Here football is regarded as a spectacle, and as Vicente Verdú points out, 'for the spectator there is no mythology or specific idolatry that could escape critical thought' (Verdú, 1980: 8). It is a conception of football as 'charged with historical mass' (*ibid*). This critical attitude involves the demythologizing of the totemic connotations of the national team as disseminated by *Abc*.

b) Heteroglot discourses integrated 'the voice of the other', in this case the unitarian discourse, as their organizing element. That is, the linguistic features of the unitarian discourse, with their appropriation of the team, their epic–nationalistic rhetoric and the values associated to it, became the centre around which the other discourses gravitated. If the unitarian concept of the Spanish nation involved unity and homogeneity, the Spanish liberal and peripheral discourses insisted on fragmentation. This was achieved by introducing heteroglossia into the discourse and by permitting 'a multiplicity of social voices' (Bakhtin, 1981: 263).

In the next sections it will be seen how by quoting the unitarian discourse, two meaning systems were generated around the terms 'past' and 'Francoism' on the one hand and 'modernity' and 'democracy' on the other. The Spanish liberal discourse generated a meaning system consisting of two categories:

jingoism/francoism/past vs patriotism/democracy/modernity

And by means of these binary oppositions, two opposite conceptions of Spain were constructed along the lines of the already mythical split of Spanish society into liberal reformists and essentialist conservatives: the Two Spains.

The disjunctive Catalanist discourse also generated a two-fold meaning system whose elements were Francoism/past vs democracy/present – but in this case the groups associated with these values were divided along territorial lines: Spain and Catalonia respectively. Both liberal and peripheral discourses heavily depended on the construction of two groups based on the dichotomy past–present. However, the difference between them lay in the consideration of which group was Francoist and stuck in the past. For the Spanish liberals this group was another part of Spanish society – the right-wing PP and its supporting media. For the disjunctive Catalanist, it was just Spain.

The Liberal Discourse: The Two Spains

'The Team of the Autonomies': The Prosification of a Symbol

El País opened up coverage of 1994 World Cup with a monographic loose magazine featuring an article by the left-wing Catalan writer Vázquez Montalbán entitled, 'La Selección de las "autonomías"' ['The Team of the "Autonomies"'] which set the tone of the coverage of this newspaper for the whole of the competition. The article reads:

The Team of the Autonomies

Insults to Clemente. Salinas was called a 'bloody Basque' and each time any player from the Basque–Catalan coalition of Barcelona Football Club touched the ball, the group of Madridist organic intellectuals sharpened their verbal attacks and showed the business card of Imperial Spain. It was said that that group of supporters were neighbours of Michel's who that way expressed their annoyance at the absence of this player from Clemente's team. But it is still curious that this group of aggressors from a residential district such as Las Rozas, where the team was staying before traveling to Canada and USA, should share the same sporting philosophy as those fanatics who filled up the Bernabéu Stadium with graffiti against Valdano and South Americans in general. The Spain of the Autonomies has turned the old arrogance of centralism into paranoia, following a process of inversion of what in a recent past was regarded as provincial 'victimism' [victim complex] against the accumulation of celebrities of the Capital.

And just in case this paranoia should be imaginary, it so happens that the Capital of the State has lost its sporting hegemony, that is, the epic hegemony of a certain conception of the State, in most sports, and the football coach proves his fundamental

Basque-centrism and a scorn for the Court [Madrid] with his sharp and unappealing manners ... If a good part of the players that make up or have made up the pre-World Cup team are Basque and Barcelona players, that is because they are part of that squad of reserves that the coach proposed to the president of Barcelona Football Club ... But for the benefit of Clemente it must be said that the Basque players he has turned to ... are the logical result of the Basque youth and reserve teams which every now and then provide undisputed players for a whole decade, in the same way as the so-called Generation of Buitre [Butrageño] was irreplaceable.

In times of fewer autonomic suspicions nobody paid attention to the number of players from the Basque Country, Catalonia or Madrid in the national team, although the coach knew how to listen to the kind requests of Don Santiago Bernabéu and thus avoid scorning his players because they were the most emblematic ones of Spain....

The Real Madrid supporters regard Michel as more Castilian than Caminero or Cañizares, because, since he is the most emblematic player of the residues of Spain One, Great and Free, his absence hurts them. Without Michel, the team smacks of an arrangement between the Catalans and the PNV [Basque Nationalist Party].

For better understanding of the text, it is important to note that the author refers to the pre-match preparation of the team before the 1994 World Cup in the residential and right-wing Madrid suburb of Las Rozas. Don Santiago Bernabéu, who fought with Franco in the Civil war and was loyal to the Francoist regime, was the President of Real Madrid between 1943 and 1978. It should be remembered that Real Madrid is regarded by many (particularly left wingers and peripheral nationalists) as 'el equipo del régimen' the team of the Francoist regime, the team of centralist Spain. The references to the Catalan–Basque coalition echo the support that the Catalan and the Basque Nationalists gave the Socialists after the 1993 General Election.

The expression 'organic intellectual' refers to the Francoist regime, which was frequently referred to by the regime itself as a 'democracia órganica'. Michel was a Real Madrid player who was not selected as part of the national team, while the term 'Madridist' is applied to supporters of Real Madrid. Valdano was at that time the Argentinian coach of Real Madrid. Butragueño was a Real Madrid player of the late eighties and early nineties. Caminero was an Atlético de Madrid player; Salinas was a Basque playing for Barcelona, and Cañizares was the reserve goalkeeper, from Valencia.

The title is significant in itself. By avoiding the term 'national', the author places the team outside the unitarian and 'eternal' dimension that the term 'nation' implies. By calling the team 'The team of the Autonomies' the object is immersed in political diversity or heteroglossia, it is given a historical dimension and it becomes related not to eternal values but to a controversial administrative and political system of the present time: the autonomic system of the Spanish State. It should be remembered here that this system replaced the highly centralized State of the Franco regime and the implication of the denomination 'the Team of the "Autonomies"' is the end of the Francoist sporting symbol. That is, the symbol of the unity of Spain is plunged into the contradictory arena of political discourse, thus marking the end of its poetic and totemic (and unitarian) status and letting it be exposed to controversy. As Bakhtin points out, a symbol cannot presuppose any fundamental relationship to another's word, to another's voice' (*ibid*: 328) (as the unitarian discourse of *Abc* did in relationship to the Spanish team). And, Bakhtin continues, 'as soon as another's voice, another's accent, the possibility of another's point of view breaks through this play of the symbol, the poetic plane is destroyed and the symbol is translated onto the plane of prose' (*ibid*: 328).

Already in the title of the article the author is attempting to prosify the team, which becomes 'a focal point for heteroglot voices' (Bakhtin, 1981: 278). The introduction of the other's voice is aimed at revealing the lack of unity around the team and presenting the territorial and ideological tensions that divide the country (contrary to what *Abc* would do). And, in fact, introducing the voice of the unitarian discourse is the first purpose of the whole article. Hence the abrupt opening of the article with a reference to someone else's words –'insults to Clemente'. It is clear that this is the voice of another (and not the author's own): *they* called Salinas a 'Bloody Basque'.

This 'they' refers to a collectivity whose identity and whose belief-system are established in the rest of the article. Vázquez Montalbán establishes a direct relationship between the utterers of these words (the heralds of state centralism) and Francoism by calling them 'the group of Madridist organic intellectuals'. Although the author acknowledges the opinion that these 'organic intellectuals' were motivated by personal reasons ('It was said that that group of supporters were neighbours of Michel's'), the sentence starting with 'but' ('But it is still curious that...') refutes this in order to give the event a political explanation justified by the supposed coincidence of the aggressors' 'sporting philosophy' with the 'racist' and 'fanatical' supporters of Real Madrid. This would become the second most important aim of the article: to encode the insults hurled against Clemente, which were generally accepted as the act of a group of barbaric Real Madrid supporters, in political terms. Apart from 'insulting', the other is 'centralist', 'intolerant' and 'imperialistic', all epithets associated with Francoism.

Furthermore, this group is assigned a temporal aspect: Imperial Spain is opposed to the Spain of the Autonomies, and in this new democratic State the old imperialists and centralists are the leftovers of a Spain of the past: 'the leftovers of Spain One, Great and Free'. Vázquez Montalbán reproduces here the myth of the two Spains in which the Francoist one is in the minority and stuck in the past. The author also launches the idea that the Francoist elements have virtually disappeared from Spain, having lost the ideological battle: 'the epic hegemony of a certain conception of the State'.

Amongst this variety of voices the author makes himself heard. His stance regarding the incontestability of Spain as a country is rather clear: territorial tensions are demoted to 'autonomic suspicions'. This idea of peaceful relationship of all the component parts of Spain (despite the 'suspicions') was also reproduced by *La Vanguardia*, which on 25 July 1994 published an article entitled 'Clemente and Azkargorta' (the Basque coach of the Bolivian team). It read: 'for the first time two Spanish coaches (or Basque coaches, if you're fussy about that kind of thing) clash in a World Cup'. Bearing in mind the political tension between the Catalan nationalists and the PP and given the fact that this newspaper is almost exclusively sold in Catalonia, the article might sound surprising, to say the least. However, one has to remember that *La Vanguardia*, as cynics might put it, is the mouthpiece of that section of Catalanism which feels sentimentally Catalan but politically and economically Spanish; that is, an undoubted defender of symbols of Catalanicity such as Catalan political institutions and language, but without renouncing its ambitions to be a major player in the Spanish context.

For both Vázquez Montalbán in *El País* and for *La Vanguardia* the unity of Spain is not brought into question. And that is the reason why, for Vázquez Montalbán, the good quality of the Catalan and Basque players justifies their selection for the national team in the same way as the Real Madrid players used to be selected before. Anything beyond this pragmatic and logical reason is 'victimism' (a feature attributed to peripheral nationalism by its detractors) or 'paranoia' (believing that the dominance of Catalan and Basque players in the team is the result of a 'Catalano-Basque coalition' or that the team is 'an arrangement between the Catalans and the PNV'). 'Victimism' and 'paranoia' are two attitudes that imply absurd fixed ideas and a persecution complex, two attitudes not based in reality (that is, the decentralized, pluralistic and multicultural reality of modern Spain). As the author notes, victimism and paranoia are two attitudes adopted by peripheral nationalists first, and now, 'in a process of inversion', by centralist Spain. Therefore, the author places these two ideologies (peripheral nationalism and centralist Spanish nationalism) in the same category, two ideologies characterized by a tendency to distort reality.

And what is the author's voice regarding 'Spanish reality'? At the end of the article Vázquez Montalbán shows no problem in accepting the team as the representative of the nation – he calls it the national team without inverted commas in the text. Therefore, the title of the article cannot be interpreted as the author's own words – that is why he distances himself from it by enclosing the term 'autonomies' within the formal indicators of another's language (the inverted commas). The temporal split between now and 'in times of fewer autonomic suspicions' implies that territorial tension is just temporal and that in normal times the team would be 'the national team'.

Vázquez Montalbán's article and the quote from *La Vanguardia* will gain more importance when the disjunctive Catalan discourse of *Avui* is dealt with. The latter discourse would not accept the idea of a Spain that has overcome its Francoist past, and become democratic and tolerant (accepting such a transformation would eliminate one of the fundamental tools for the delegitimation of Madrid power). In *Avui*'s discourse territorial tension is not the product of groundless 'suspicions' that vary with the political atmosphere, but the result of historically different value systems.

Jingoistic Hooliganism vs Civilized Patriotism

The division of Spanish society in two groups (the Two Spains) seen in Vázquez Montalbán's article, was also developed (albeit in an aggressive and elitist tone) by Francisco Umbral (*El Mundo*, 5 July 1994). This time 'the other' is not a particular group of Real Madrid supporters but, indeed, the common supporters of the Spanish national team, which were constructed according to the image of the supporter promoted by the unitarian media. That is, Francisco Umbral was criticizing what *Abc* was promoting.

In the text, Francisco Umbral speaks about the reaction of some Spanish football fans who, in the Madrid celebrations of the victory of the team over Switzerland (these celebrations traditionally take place in the Plaza de Cibeles, in central Madrid) cut off one of the arms of the statue of the goddess of Agriculture, Cibeles, which holds the keys to the city. The amputated arm was missing for some days and later found. Contrary to the previous article, the voices of these supporters (called at one point 'españistas', a term explained below) are not reproduced; therefore their actions are the only factor used to portray their identity. The absence of the words of these *españistas* is of extreme importance for the significance of the text and will be explained below:

> Cibeles had her arm cut off, with the keys to the city, by the hooligans of soccer patriotism, the stupid supporters, the Spanish teleloonies. On the night of the victory I was walking around Madrid surrounded by crazy waves of horns, and I was thinking that there is no spectacle as dumb as this unmotivated, gratuitous and depressing joy. How sad you get with the joy of idiots, whether in the lunatic asylum, or at football or on telly...

> Everything that goes through television degrades; and from this tele-degradation of showbiz football springs the agraphic joy of the idiots, the destructive happiness of the mediocre. It's what Ortega defined, quoting another, as "the vertical invasion of the vandals". The vandals come from the tacky underground world of television culture – they see a goddess and they cut her arm off. What I tell my sport colleagues is that I'm begging for Spain to lose all her matches; or that someone else knocks us out of this World Cup because, if every victory is going to

mean a chip off Madrid, at the end we'll have the Cup and twice the bloody cup, but the city will be left looking like when Franco took it.

What I mean is that if this shitty World Cup doesn't finish soon or if we don't get knocked out ... the supporters, the *torcida*, the fans, the crowd, the remote control *españistas*, will win the bloody Cup for us, but they will leave Madrid looking like at the time of the French invasion.

Socialist culture, which used to be a real culture, has been turned by the PSOE into national team Francoist culture, with the support of the five or whatever channels churning out football matches, eagerly turning the crowd into zombies.

The theme of the divide in Spanish society in this article is compounded by other themes such as the degrading effect of football and, more specifically, televised football. On the surface, televised football degradation seems to be only indirectly related to the subject of media constructions of national identity. But the link is clear if we contrast the portrait of the national supporters in this text with that of the sport dailies such as *Marca*, *As*, and, more significantly, the conservative *Abc*. A look around those newspapers shows that the denunciation of the barbaric attitude of the supporters who committed the act of amputation of the statue, was evident right across the media board. However, *Marca*, *As* and *Abc* did not put down this urge to celebrate and to cause havoc to 'soccer patriotism' – that is, they did not provide a political explanation. In fact, as seen above, *Abc* actually glorified sport nationalism by using the image of the unity of expectant and patriotic Spaniards sitting in front of their television sets, and demonstrating their joy for the victories of the team. In the *El Mundo* article, however, the relationship between the attitude of the joyful Spanish supporters and the excesses of their 'soccer patriotism' is pivotal.

The idea of degraded patriotism is reinforced by 'españista', a neologism invented *ad hoc* by the author. The closest existing adjective to 'españista' is 'españolista', currently used to pejoratively name the defenders of 'españolismo', another pejorative term for the political conception of Spain close to traditional centralism. By inventing this neologism, the author deprives the supporters of any political motivation or purpose. Their team is *España*, therefore they are 'españistas'; in the same way as supporters of Barcelona F.C are called 'barcelonistas', and supporters of Real Madrid 'madridistas'. Their 'patriotism' is, therefore, politically void. Furthermore, one of the denotations of the suffix '-ismo' and '-ista' (like their English counterparts, '-ism' and '-ist') is adherence to a principle. In the final analysis, these Spanish patriotic supporters (who correspond to the image of the supporter as constructed by the unitarian media) are depicted as partisans, but partisans with no political aim.

That is the reason why the supporters, according to the author, are 'stupid' (the original Spanish 'tonto' refers to a person of little intelligence in the general acceptation, and 'mentally weak' in the psychiatric sense); and stupid with no objective, hence the description of their sport happiness as 'unmotivated, gratuitous and depressing joy', 'the joy of idiots'. Therefore, their patriotism is, by association, also unmotivated, gratuitous and depressing. Although the supporters are portrayed as 'patriotic', the association with 'soccer' turns them rather into a jingoistic bunch.

In typical elitist fashion, the supporters are not only deprived of intellectual attributes, but also they are represented as a thing – they are an object of display to be looked at, hence the reference to the action of the collective other as a 'spectacle'. In linguistic terms, they remain outside the 'correlation of personality' (Benveniste, 1971: 200) formed by I (the author) and you (the reader). It is worth developing here this linguistic point. In his studies on the notion of 'person' in both verbs and pronouns Benveniste concludes that '"I/you" possesses the sign of person; "he" lacks it'. The "third person" has, with respect to the form itself, the constant characteristic and function of representing a nonpersonal invariant, and nothing but that' (*ibid*). Benveniste further observes that:

> "I" designates the one who speaks and at the same time implies an utterance about "I". In saying "I" I cannot *not* be speaking of myself. In the second person, "you" is necessarily designated by "I" and cannot be thought of outside a situation set up by starting with "I"; and at the same time, "I" states something as the predicate of "you". But in the third person a predicate is really stated, only it is outside "I–you"; this form is thus an exception to the relationship by which "I" and "you" are specified. Consequently, the legitimacy of this form as a "person" is to be questioned (1971: 197).

The consequence of this observation is that 'the "third person" is not a "person"; it is really the verbal form whose function is to express the non-person' (ibid: 198). This blunt reification (understood here as transformation into a thing) and display of the supporters, places them in a clearly opposite position to the author and his reader. The supporters become looked at from an external perspective.

Precisely because this patriotic bunch of supporters are a 'thing', they are represented by their actions and not by their speech. Umbral does not let them speak, unlike Vázquez Montalbán in his article. Umbral only lets them act. This difference is important. Bakhtin, on considering the activity of any character in the novel, states that it is 'always ideologically demarcated: he lives and acts in an ideological world of his own ... he has his own perception of the world that is incarnated in his action and his discourse' (Bakhtin, 1981: 335). However, as Bakhtin points out, it is 'impossible to reveal through the character's acts, and through these acts alone, his ideological position and the ideological world at its heart without representing his discourse' (*ibid*). And this is a key point in the article analysed here: the author does not let his characters speak because, besides being hooligans, stupid supporters, teleloonies, destructive, mediocre, tacky, vandals, and lacking a concrete ideology, they suffer from 'agraphia', that is, they are unable to express something in writing due to a brain injury. The source of agraphia is the degrading effect of television and its consequence, the attitude of the supporters, including their football patriotism.

From the point of view of this analysis, agraphia is the essential feature of the supporters, the source of their action. It is also the feature that splits the society constructed in the text: against this barbaric background, the author incorporates the world of culture in the figure of Ortega y Gasset (the other great regenerationist intellectual together with Unamuno). As corresponds to the world of culture, the philosopher is allowed to speak: 'It's what Ortega defined, quoting another, as "the vertical invasion of the vandals"'. Francisco Umbral lets Ortega y Gasset utter an opinion and both become situated within the same value system.

Furthermore, the section of Spain depicted here in the figure of the supporters and their television instigators, is not only wild (hence the identification of the supporters with the French invaders of the early nineteenth century) and uncultured, but also the heirs of Francoism. That is how the sentence 'if every victory is going to mean a chip off Madrid, at the end we'll have the Cup and twice the bloody cup, but the city will be left looking like when Franco took it' should be interpreted. The identification of national enthusiasm with Francoism and lack of culture is more evident when the author expresses his final denunciation of the Socialist government: 'Socialist culture, which used to be a real culture, has been turned by the PSOE into national team Francoist culture, with the support of the five or whatever channels churning out football matches, very keenly turning the crowd into zombies'. It is interesting to note the link established between the PSOE and Francoism, which goes to show that associations with Francoist ideology is a strategy used across the political spectrum in Spain to de-legitimize political rivals. In Umbral's article the Socialist party and its media (the state-run television channels) are included as agents of a degrading nationalistic discourse, not surprisingly so, given the aggressive stance that the daily *El Mundo* (where this article appeared) took against the PSOE and in support of the Partido Popular after the 1994 European elections.

This article is a clear instance of the rejection of the promotion of nationalism through sport. In it (as in the article by Vázquez Montalbán analysed above), two groups are again constructed: the other, who is barbaric, un-cultured, un-civilized and Francoist; and the author's own group of culture and civilization, and, one may argue, civilized patriotism. The use of culture and civilization as the distinguishing factor between the two groups and the incorporation of the words of Ortega y Gasset makes the myth of the two Spains sound again. It destroys the myth of national unity and, finally, parodies the efforts to create national enthusiasm through football.

The Differential Discourse

The differential discourse was not widely disseminated during the 1994 World Cup, and one could only identify a few articles and comments. It can be argued that in a period of territorial tension and constant attacks on Catalanism (mainly from *Abc* and *El Mundo*), *La Vanguardia* (the main conduit of moderate Catalanism) chose to remain largely outside this debate in relation to football (though not necessarily in other parts of the newspaper).

In fact, the most emblematic 'differential' article one could find did not appear in *La Vanguardia* but in *El País*, signed, not altogether unexpectedly, by a Catalan journalist, Santiago Segurola. The emphasis of that article was on the historic and symbolic dimension of the team as a 'peripheral' (although still Spanish) phenomenon representative of the plural Spain, given the small number of players from Real Madrid. In the match versus Bolivia no players from Real Madrid took part and Santiago Segurola in his article 'Sueños' ('Dreams') (*El País*, 29 June 1994) wrote:

> The line-up had another symbolic reading, an oddity in the
> history of the team. No player from Real Madrid appeared in
> the line-up. It was a peripheral line-up, a team that broke all
> the preconceived stylistic and historical moulds.

This welcoming of a 'peripheral' team was not so enthusiastic in *Avui*, where the line-up was not 'a dream', but a curiosity: 'One would have to search through the files to find something similar, if there's ever been one, because we can't find any' (*Avui*, 30 June 1994), said *Avui* rather dispassionately.

Apart from this short example, one could not find any textual reproduction of the differential discourse. This discourse will be looked into in detail in chapter 3 which covers the process of agreement between CiU and the PP after the March 1996 general election. At that moment the possibility of a pact between the Catalanists and the Popular Party eased the confrontation ruling Spanish politics and left the door open for a full-blown expression of the differential discourse.

The Disjunctive Discourse

In line with the other dailies regarded here as heteroglot, *Avui* placed the reader in the position of spectator in relation to the team, following the rules of objective journalism. However, *Avui* never called the players 'our players' or the team 'our team' and never involved its readers in the actions of the team. This distance allowed an interpretation of the team in its historical dimension in an attempt to demythicize it. As noted earlier, revealing the 'historical mass' of the team was also one of the features of the liberal discourse. However, the analysis of a disjunctive text from *Avui* carried out in this section will reveal key differences between both discourses. For the liberal discourse, the quasi-Manichean division of Spain into two groups also opens up the possibility of redemption and regeneration: we have seen how for Vázquez Montalbán this regeneration has already started and the Francoist and almost barbaric Spain is just the 'leftovers' of the recent past; likewise, Umbral's insistence on culture leaves the door, at least theoretically, open for renewal. The disjunctive discourse, by contrast, depicted a Spain of only one face closing up the possibility of regeneration. And while in the liberal discourse detachment from the team and its victories was due to ideological reasons, the disjunctive discourse rejected the team not only on ideological but also on territorial grounds. In that sense Anton M. Espalder expressed his opinion of why he was against the World Cup:

> I don't want to refer to the poor quality of the broadcasts because it's obvious and incomprehensible. Nor to the group of commentators, committed to proving ... [that] football is very primitive. Even less to the bonfire of patriotic fanaticism that it caused to the South West and beyond, and which is felt by many as a constant reminder to renew your passport (*Avui*, 3 July 1994).

The articles analysed in previous sections established a two-sided split within Spanish society and attributed jingoism to a conservative 'other'. For the disjunctive discourse, jingoism is a feature of Spanish society as a whole, as opposed to Catalan society – a dividing territorial line between Catalonia and 'the South West and beyond' that separates two different societies.

These elements were present in the article 'El Partit de la Germanor' ('The Match of the Brotherhood') by Bru Noya, which appeared in *Avui* on 2 July 1994, one day before the match against Switzerland. I will analyse this article in depth, but for better understanding of the text some historical and circumstantial references should be explained.

The period was rife with political corruption, hence the reference to the Director of the Civil Guard Luís Roldán, who had disappeared after being accused of the embezzlement of very large sums of money. J. V. Foix will be mentioned: he is a Catalan poet (b.1893, d.1987) whose earliest collections of prose poems are narratives which 'seem to take place in the frontiers of the dream' but constitute 'a waking dream in which the poet never abandons his control' (Terry, 1999: 193). *Hortxata* is a white drink made from tiger nuts typical of the Valencian and Catalan area, what Catalanists call the *Països Catalans* – Catalan nations. *Hortxata* is sold in J. V. Foix's cafeteria in Sarriá, a wealthy quarter of Barcelona. The adjective 'Ortegan' refers to the Spanish liberal regenerationist Ortega y Gasset. There is also a reference to the Tour de France, which in 1994 clashed with the Football World

Cup. Indurain, the Spanish cyclist from Navarre, and Rominger, a Swiss cyclist are also mentioned in the text. The reference to 'gold' is to the gold reserves which the Government of the Republic sent to Moscow during the Civil War and which Spain never recovered.

It must be remembered that the original article is in Catalan, except for the expression 'Episodio Nacional' which appears in Castilian. The implications of this language switch will be dealt with in the analysis of the text. For the sake of clarity, it should be noted that 'Episodio Nacional' is a reference to the vast work of the nineteenth-century writer Benito Pérez Galdós, *Episodios Nacionales*, a chronicle of the history of nineteenth-century Spain, full of collective characters who proclaim the power of the Spanish nation. The article reads:

> Although Epicurus agreed that the wise man must stay calm and in control of himself, even in his dreams, you who prefer our own things would rather remember J.V. Foix and his 'it's when I dream that I see clearly'.
>
> Because it's then that, after one of those nice glasses of *hortxata* like the ones they sell in his cafeteria, you will abandon yourself to sleep which will take you to bucolic landscapes ... and you will dream of a country like Switzerland. There are other sleepyheads who dream of Switzerland – but they dream of the money they already have in its banks or they would like to have there.
>
> These very same people will shout against the Swiss when they wake up, linking the World Cup and tonight's match with the Tour de France and the Indurain–Rominger duel; those same people who will demand, just like new Ortegan 1898 regenerationists, a new *National Episode*, like the one during the 1964 European Cup. Then, at the Santiago Bernabéu Stadium in Madrid, Marcelino's goal against the Soviet Union was used by the whole of Spanishness, the Spanishness of twenty five years of peace [this is how Francoism referred to the period from 1939 to 1964] and trade union demonstrations on the first of May [Fascist-style demonstrations celebrating the Francoist Regime], to take revenge for the affront of the gold that fled to Moscow during the Civil War. All in all, that

> was a mere trifle compared to what those who now proclaim their
> patriotic spirit to all and sundry [Roldán] have taken out.

> The long-awaited match ... between the Spaniards and the Swiss
> should be a display of brotherhood and good co-existence. Maybe
> between the two of them they will find a way to make Roldán, a
> good client of the Swiss banks, appear once and for all...

The text starts by introducing polyphony of voices by quoting the word of another and putting it aside later on. Despite the self-control suggested by Epicurus as the feature of the wise man, the author of the article would rather quote J. V. Foix's aphorism of an identical spirit of control even when dreaming. The author seems to be saying 'why quote someone else if we have our own Catalan thinker who has said exactly the same?' That way the text seems to perform a zoom-in from the universality of the Greek philosopher's truth to the local truth. A truth that is valid for all Catalans since it echoes the concept *seny*, which, as noted above, encapsulates values such as common sense, moderation, and rationalism; and by contrast is the opposite of dogmatism and lack of control.

The first two paragraphs are characterized by a type of communication situation described as 'experiential' by Lyons (1977b: 668), which implies the personal involvement of the speaker, a situation in which 'I' and 'you' are explicitly designated 'here' and 'now'. In the first paragraph the author constructs and describes his reader as someone who prefers local things ('our own things') and accepts J. V. Foix's aphorism as his/her own.

This solidarity effect created by the conversational form of the text is reinforced by the use of the informal variant of second-person pronoun, (*tu* in the Catalan original) which the author uses to address his reader. As Trudgill states following Roger Brown and Albert Gilman:

it seems that the usage of V [which stands for Vous, the formal second-person pronoun in French], which when employed by the power-less to the power-full signified a difference of power, became generalized to symbolize all types of social difference and distance. As a result of this new factor, T-usage now became more probable when the degree of intimacy, similarity or solidarity between speakers was felt to be quite large ... Solidarity presumably because of the gradual rise of democratic egalitarian ideology, has today become the major factor involved (Trudgill, 1993: 103).

The first paragraph also includes one of the main elements of the disjunctive discourse: the territorial dimension in the split between characters. In his own article, Francisco Umbral, despite the clear distance established in relation to the jingoistic supporters depicted in his text, necessarily shares the same urban space with them. However, Bru Noya establishes a territorial delimitation by means of the introduction of the deictic 'here'. This is a spatial dimension, a specific geographical place where only 'I' and 'you' are included, and where the collective Catalan identity of these characters is further defined by an action of 'you': to have *hortxata* in J. V. Foix's café in Sarrià – a Catalan drink in a Catalan place.

The second paragraph fulfils a two-fold function. Firstly, the introductory 'because' opens the way to an explanation of the contents of the aphorism, which in this case implies an action: maintaining self-control in dreams. Furthermore, these are nice dreams which transport the dreamer to 'bucolic' spots and construct a Catalan character with a tranquil and clear conscience. These elements echo two of the key legitimating symbols of Catalan self-perception: 'the tranquil periphery' and 'the Catalan oasis'. Secondly, the causal conjunction 'because' explains away and endorses the aphorism. This act of justification of the words of Foix creates a common background shared by the reader and the author, a cultural consensus. The aphorism is, therefore, taken as the common view, that is, it includes the point of view and the value system regarded as normal by a society. This second paragraph constitutes, thus, an act of consolidation of the community.

The correlation 'I/you' and 'here' is brusquely contrasted by a third person ('there are other sleepyheads who ...') whose actions are completely different. Just as in the previous text by Francisco Umbral, 'I/you' form an explicit 'correlation of personality' (Benveniste, 1971: 200) from which 'them' remain excluded and become objectified, reified. In order to better define this 'other' the author plays with an ambiguity, and then with a clarification: the dreams of Switzerland are given two opposing connotations whereby the tranquil and bucolic dream of the reader is contrasted with the suspicious financial dreams of the others.

And who are the 'others'? Their identity takes on a clear definite shape in the third paragraph where the following meaning system takes form:

1) the corrupt politicians become associated with the Spanish patriots: 'These very same people will shout against the Swiss...' and 'those people who now proclaim their patriotic spirit to all and sundry'.

2) The relationship between football and patriotism is ridiculed, just as in Umbral's text above. However, there is a conspicuous difference between the two texts: Umbral's places the ideology of regenerationism as a guarantee of the transformation and betterment of Spanish society. In contrast, in Bru Noya's text (as representative of the Catalan disjunctive discourse) the idea of 1898 regenerationism (with a special mention of Ortega y Gasset although he did not belong to the 1898 generation of intellectuals and artists) is parodied. How is it parodied? By means of an exaggerated comparison that attempts to depoliticise, trivialize and demote the regenerationist ideology to a demand for a sporting feat: a National Episode.

3) The new regenerationist 'Episodio Nacional' is not only parodied but also becomes associated with the Francoist past by means of the comparison 'like the one during the 1964 European Cup', and the references to the Franco regime: 'the twenty five years of peace' (which is the way Francoist regime referred to the period between the end of the war until 1964), 'the trade union demonstrations on the first of May' (turned by Franco into a self-glorifying show), and the 'revenge for the affront of the gold that fled to Moscow during the Civil War'.

Apart from these associations and comparisons, the set of verb tenses in this paragraph also plays a key role in the construction of the identity of the others. The future tense that introduces the paragraph ('will shout against the Swiss') indicates the certainty that the character will act in a particular known way. As Benveniste indicates for the French future tense (also applicable to its Catalan counterpart), 'it is only a present projected towards the future; it implies prescription, obligation and certitude, which are subjective modalities, not historical categories' (1971: 211).

This certainty about the future actions of the others is based on what their actions in the past have allegedly been. And it is interesting to note how the explanation of that past is rendered in the particular type of 'historical' communication situation (as opposed to 'experiential' used until now). On the one hand, in this section of the paragraph all forms of autobiographical linguistic forms are brusquely excluded. The pronouns 'I' and 'you' completely disappear from the text and the two main verbs are in the preterite and the pluperfect. The fresh, full-blooded and near-to-speech style whereby reality is constructed in all its density (Barthes, 1984: 28), used in the previous paragraphs is replaced in this section by the use of the preterite. And here the preterite constructs a reality that is reduced to 'a slim and pure logos, without density, without volume, without spread' (*ibid*). In this reality, the football victory against the Soviet Union in 1964, the patriotic enthusiasm it provoked and the pathetic revenge of Spain for the gold it claimed back from Russia, are all linked without volume, all given the same importance and identified with the ideology of the regenerationists.

A relationship between the past and the present is established here. The author seems to be asserting that 'we know how they acted then and we can be sure of their future behaviour'. The past and future actions of 'them' become crystal clear and predictable. And this predictability implies yet another feature of 'them': their lack of evolution and their permanence in an everlasting past – the Franco regime. The message is 'they acted like that in 1964 and they will act the same thirty years later'. In the final analysis, the others are constructed as corrupt, patriotic, Francoist and hopelessly irregenerable.

Furthermore, if at the beginning the 'others' only seemed to include a group of corrupt politicians, at the end of the text it is clear that it refers to all Spaniards (i.e. non-Catalans) in the phrase 'the whole of Spanishness'. Moreover, the reader and author are excluded from this national group in the final paragraph where the Spaniards are treated as 'them': 'The long-awaited match ... between the Spaniards and the Swiss should be a display of brotherhood and good coexistence. Maybe between the two of them they will find a way...'

In order to reinforce the disparity between both groups, Spanish and Catalan, disjunctive discourse constructs a monolithic and one-dimensional identity of the 'others' by means of a kind of metonymy (in the same way as the unitarian discourse used the 'one nation, one team' metonymy). In this text the attitudes of a minority group (corrupt politicians) are presented as the norm in Spanish society;

71

and the attitude and words of the poet J. V. Foix as representative of Catalan society. In that way, any differences and struggles within those societies are passed over following the 'principle of metacontrast' (Hogg and McGarthy, 1990: 14), a process that consists in maximizing the intercategorial differences and minimizing the intracategorial ones.

These metonymies have a clear political intention. Studies on intergroup contact have shown that 'increasing the perceived variability of an out-group should decrease the tendency to treat all group members in a similar negative way' (Johnson and Hewstone, 1990: 199). And in the particular case of the text analysed here, the contrary is precisely the objective: the construction of out-group members (Spaniards) as similar to one another, makes it easier to treat them all in a similar, typically negative way. Treating the out-group in such a manner also 'preserves the status and social identity of the in-group' (*ibid*: 201).

Linguistic Switch and National Boundaries

The dividing line between Spaniards and Catalans is reinforced by the only use of the Castilian language in the whole text, the parodical 'Episodio Nacional'. In a previous study (León Solís and O'Donnell, 1994), the ideological use of one particular language in bilingual societies like Catalonia was examined. Following the classification of different kinds of bilingualism carried out by Kremnitz (1992: 37–74), it was established that the Catalan case is intrinsic rather than extrinsic. In cases of extrinsic (or territorial) bilingualism as in Belgium, two linguistic communities live side by side but there is little everyday need to use or even know the language of the other community. In the case of Catalonia, the bulk of the inhabitants (in particular those born in Catalonia) are able to understand and speak both Castilian and Catalan. In a situation such as this, the choice of language can be more than a case of mere 'code-switching', the free and systematic use of the two languages depending on circumstances. The conscious choice of language or a switch from one language to another can acquire an ideological complexity which is absent in communities characterized by monolingualism or extrinsic bilingualism: the use of either Castilian or Catalan opens an ideological dimension which the use of the other closes off, particularly when they appear in the very same text.

Let's clarify this point with an example from the front-page headline of the Valencian magazine (written in Valencian Catalan), *El Temps,* of 28 February

1994. Beneath the short lead in small letters and in Catalan 'Membres de la Brigada Político-Social franquista encara manen', (Members of the Francoist Politico-social Brigade still rule) the title read in medium-sized letters also in Catalan 'ELS TORTURADORS DE SEMPRE' (the same old torturers). Beneath those two sentences there figured the single word in large letters and in Castilian: '¡Presentes!'. 'Presentes' is an expression meaning 'still live' which was most notably uttered after the name of the two dictators Primo de Rivera and Franco after their deaths. The use of Castilian for the term '¡Presentes!' instantly associates torture with *Spanish* army and dictators, and dissociates Catalonia (or the *països catalans*) from involvement in such practices.

The text being analysed here constitutes a similar case. The expression *Episodio Nacional* could also have been used in an ironic way by detractors of Spanish sports jingoism in line with the liberal regenerationist ideology – writers such as Francisco Umbral or Váquez Montalbán. However, the use of Castilian here has a 'symbolic boundary-function' (Fishman, 1989: 35) whereby the distinction between the two separate Catalan and Spanish identities is reinforced. The use of *Episodi nacional* (in Catalan) instead of the Castilian *Episodio nacional* would have closed off the ideological dimension of the Castilian expression used in a completely Catalan context; it would have hindered, if not prevented, the clear distinction between 'us' and 'them' in terms of national identities.

4. Myths and Counter-mythical Myths

It has been seen that the conservative daily *Abc*, regarded here as the most representative reproducer of the unitarian discourse, excluded politics from national football team talk and stripped it off its historical dimension. This exclusion had a clear political aim. The relationship with the reader following the Spanish team's performance was built upon fostering a sense of identification with a national symbol and even partisanship. The defence of national unity was also behind the exclusion of heteroglossia (the words of others) from the unitarian discourse for two interrelated reasons: a) in order to avoid reference to fragmenting issues, such as ideological and territorial strife, which might have made void the unifying function of one of the last emblems of national unity – the national team; and b) in order to avoid introducing voices that might have made this discourse crumble; that is, to prevent 'dialogization', which is in itself an index that 'a word, discourse, language or culture ... becomes relativized' (Bakhtin, 1981: 427).

Against the strength of a unitary verbal-ideological world of national coherence constructed around the 'nation-team' metonymy, the agents of heteroglot discourses forced forward the introduction of 'politics-in-sport and sport-as-politics' (Rowe, 1996: 105), thereby highlighting the historical and political dimension of sport and attempting to eliminate the mythical and totemic connotations of the team. Contrary to the politically motivated absence of conflict, heteroglot discourses promoted their own conceptions of Spain as fundamentally fragmented by means of a dichotomizing practice consisting of the introduction of the voice of the other, more specifically, the voice of the unitarian discourse typical of *Abc*. The latter became objectified, transformed into 'the subject of communication, interpretation, discussion, evaluation [and] rebuttal' (Bakhtin, 1981: 337). The resisting power of heteroglot discourses was expressed by recognizing 'conflict of interest' (Fiske, 1987: 316) and proposing 'multiplicity over singularity' (*ibid*).

It must be noted, however, that in all heteroglot discourses (those of *El País*, *La Vanguardia*, some articles in *El Mundo* and *Avui*), multiplicity was in fact limited to a dichotomy. Discourses with a polemic structure exploited the spatial dichotomy 'here' and 'there', each one invested with opposing values. In the case of Catalanist disjunctive discourse of *Avui* the spatial cleavage referred to the metaphoric (and widespread) images of the 'Catalan oasis' or the 'tranquil periphery' (not mentioned in the articles but clearly evoked). These two images refer not only to the tranquility of the place 'Catalonia' (with all that 'tranquility' implies in political terms – social cohesion, absence of political feuds) but also to the people, who live in 'convivència'. This 'convivència' translates approximately into English as 'co-existence', though the notion of actually 'living side by side' in harmony and forming one coherent whole is much more to the fore in the Catalan term. In Catalonia, 'Convivència' is widely accepted as one of the dominant features of Catalan identity. Indeed, the 'Catalanicity' that this notion conveys is so strong that the very accusation of a lack of commitment to it, is tantamount to an accusation of being un-Catalan.

All the central elements of this particularly Catalan 'convivència' can be used in order to define Catalonia in relationship to the rest of the Spanish State, which supposedly lacks them. These elements are tolerance and an ability to integrate others, a general tendency towards consensus shown in all walks of private and public life; and a commitment to democratic values. If the 'here' is a place of harmonious 'conviència', the 'there' (the place of the Spaniards) by negative definition, is defined as the opposite of tranquillity, harmony and democracy. This spatial divide points to the distinction between 'us' Catalans and 'them' Spaniards with no common space to share, no common national identity.

Dichotomous segmentation was also one of the most important features of both liberal and disjunctive discourses during the coverage of the 1994 Football World Cup. Indeed, the heteroglot discourses performed an act of demythicism – they were 'counter-mythical' (Barthes, 1972: 136). Whereas the Unitarian myth of the team and the nation eliminated all contradictions and divides, the liberal and Catalanist discourses immersed them in the hubbub of political relations and actions.

Notwithstanding this, having repoliticized the team and other symbols of national identity, having acted as counter-mythical discourses, the final product was another myth. Liberal and disjunctive Catalanist discourses might have attempted to counter-attack the mythic metanarrative of Spain *One, Great and Free*, but the heterogeneity they proposed was very limited. The black and white distinction between 'us' and 'them' in both discourses was nothing but a myth, a purification of things – to use Roland Barthes's idea in *Mythologies* (1972: 143). Just as the unitarian discourse did, the liberal and disjunctive discourses 'abolish[ed] the complexity' (*ibid*) of Spanish and Catalan societies, and gave things 'the simplicity of essences' (*ibid*). Despite the show of ideological struggle, they did 'away with all dialectics' (*ibid*) and organized 'a world which [was] without contradictions' (*ibid*), other than the contradictions between 'us' and 'them' expressed in the mythical constructions of the Two Spains or the disjunctive interpretation of the relationship between Spain and Catalonia.

5. Epilogue. From Opposition to Consensus

The first legs of the 2002 World Cup were particularly good for the Spanish team. In the first round it played and beat all three members of its group: Slovenia (2 June) – the first time Spain won its first match in a World Cup for five decades, Paraguay (7 June) and South Africa (12 June). In the second round the Spanish team beat Ireland (16 June) on penalties, to be finally beaten by South Korea in the quarter-finals amid accusations of favouritism by the referees for the local team.

This time the controversies present in 1994 were all but absent. In the sporting field, the coach Camacho was not particularly polemical. And at a political level the pact between CiU and the PP let the controversy between centre and periphery, and consequently, the debate about the identity of Spain, be put on the back burner. It was a time of 'fewer autonomic suspicions', to use Vázquez Montalbán's words from 1994. This new situation had an effect on the form of and interaction between the discourses of national identity: the dialogical and agonistic form of texts was all but abandoned (except in *Avui*). If in 1994 the use of the first-person plural to refer to the team was a point of contention, now it was widespread and generalized (albeit to different degrees). Likewise, some the main features of *Abc*'s rhetoric – the representation of a united Spanish people behind their team, and the defence of 'Spanish patriotism' and of a unifying all-Spanish 'national feeling' was present in all dailies (again to different degrees and with the exception of *Avui*, which insisted that the Spanish team is not their team and warned its readers of the 'primitive jingoism' that the team generates).

Let's give some examples. The journalist Antonio Burgos spoke of the Football team as 'Our team' (*El Mundo*, 3 June 2002); and the poet Eduardo Mendicutti calls the players 'our boys' (*El Mundo*, 3 June 2002). The day after the difficult match against Ireland, *El Mundo* reserved the privileged space of its editorial to describe the match of the Spanish team ('our team') in epic terms, which in Spain, as noted, is regarded as reminiscent of Francoist rhetoric and more typical of a sports daily or *Abc*: 'we faced extra time with two players less' but finally 'fate sided with *us*' (my italics). And for columnists in *El País*, this time round the team was 'our beloved team' (Ramón Irigoyen, 31 May 2002). Even in *El País*'s leading article of the day after the defeat by South Korea, the paper allowed itself to use the first-person plural that was so fiercely criticized in 1994: 'we deserved a lot more' (23 June 2002). This controversial feature aligned *El País* (usually self-contained in matters of patriotism) with *Abc*, one of whose daily columnists wrote before the match against Paraguay in defence of the use of the first person: 'what are we going to do? Like that, in the first person ... which is the best way of defining the supporters, all of the Spaniards, when dealing with the national team' (Rafael Marichalar, 6 June 2002).

This image of one people united around a national team was propped up by references to the number of supporters following the Spanish matches. For Marichalar, it is 'millions of Spaniards that support and make football possible, anxious for a heroic performance' (*Abc*, 6 June 2002). After the match against Paraguay the sports editing team of *Abc* reinforced the construction of a 'Spain, paralyzed' following the match (8 June 2002). This image was repeated across the board: *La Vanguardia* in its editorial comment wrote: 'no less than 10 million Spaniards, probably some more, got up early ... to watch ... the elimination of Spain' (23 June 2002). Juan Cruz, in *El País*, described not only Madrid, but, more controversially, Barcelona as 'deserted and as if swept by a tornado' all 'because of the team'. And he finishes his article with the rather respectful: 'Spain? Do not disturb her. She's re-united celebrating her victory' (13 June 2002). In the Spanish original the word used is *reunida*, which can mean 'at a meeting' and, more interestingly, 're-united', giving an idea of new unity and even psychological bonding. Furthermore, the warning to leave Spain alone echoes a desire not to spoil the spell of unity with controversies, at least for a while.

In *La Vanguardia* and *El País* there was some debate about the support or loathing that the Spanish team generates in Catalonia. It is important to note that the Spanish High Court had decided that Catalan sport teams (including the football team) were not entitled to take part in international events, but only in friendly matches. In both newspapers, the stance taken was for the compatibility of supporting both teams. The regular columnist of *El País*, Sergi Pamiès (a Catalan), took the line of the 'Double Fatherland' and wrote: 'the funny thing is that, independently of what should be logic, one can love both teams at the same time without being mad and even when both teams are, theoretically, incompatible' (19 June 2002). Enric Bañeres, in *La Vanguardia*, pointed out that it might be 'understandable' and 'acceptable' for some to be against the Spanish team because it is 'imposed on them and represents them by force', but, Bañeres went on, 'it is legitimate and very respectable that others feel happy and content when Puyol, Casillas [Barcelona F.C players] and company win' (21 June 2002). Taking things a little further, for Javier Cercas (a writer from Extremadura) those who support other international teams rather than the Spanish one (not uncommon in Catalonia when Spain plays, in the same way as many Scots support England's rivals) are moved by 'an impossible snobbery' (*El País*, 7 June 2002).

But not everyone supported Spain. In *La Vanguardia*, despite this general tendency to support the team, there was, of course, room for some criticism of the way the World Cup was being covered by the media. Manuel Trallero, one of the few anti-Spanish team journalists of *La Vanguardia*, wrote an article entitled 'If only Spain lost', wishing Spain's defeat in order to prevent the 'hemorrhage of patriotism and the national dribble' that victories supposedly produce in the Madrid media (2 June 2002). As a clear index of the 'dialogical' nature of the matter, two articles were written in response to this one. One in support of Trallero's wishful thinking in

Avui, in an article entitled 'Long live Trallero!' (17 June 2002). Another (a compensatory one) in *La Vanguardia* itself entitled: 'If only Spain won' (4 June 2002), which was more in line with the stance of the paper.

Vázquez Montalbán (so critical of the Francoist traces in Spanish society) also wrote this time that he could 'see a certain rebirth of the Imperial epic tone in the broadcasting of the match' (*El País*, 15 June 2002); and he even described Spanish Television as a newborn 'single, universal destiny' (the Francoist description for Spain) (*El País*, 29 June 2002). However, his indictments against the 'leftovers' of Francoism, as he put it in 1994, were not as fierce as on that occasion. Also from *El País*, another Catalan writer, Enrique Vila-Matas, replied to Camacho's words that the match against Ireland had been 'epic', with: 'epic? It's clear that time does not pass' (18 June 2002) in reference to a supposed renewal of Francoist rhetoric. But these criticisms (aimed at the less conformist section of each daily's readership) amounted to very little when compared to the majority of opinion columns and editorials of the papers. They amounted to almost nothing when compared to the 1994 indictments.

In 2002 part of the French Roland Garros tennis Championship took place during the World Cup, with the particularity that three Spaniards were present in the semifinals. The final was between the Catalan Albert Costa (who won the title) and the Valencian Juan Carlos Ferrero. Valencia is part of what Catalanists call *països Catalans* (Catalan nations); however, (or precisely because of that) the interpretation of the event was unanimous in all newspapers: it was yet another Spanish final and the players were 'links in the chain of Spanish tennis' (*El País*, 10 June 2002). In headlines, *El Mundo* announced that 'Spain takes over Paris for the third time', in a match depicted as a 'national duel' (8 June 2002). From Barcelona, *La Vanguardia* also made it clear in one of its leading articles that it was another 'Spanish final', 'the third one in the last nine years...' (9 June 2002). But probably the most exaggeratedly patriotic interpretation of the event was that of *Abc* which called it in headlines a 'New apotheosis of Spanish tennis' (8 June 2002).

If all the dailies coincided in representing the event as a 'Spanish final', this sense of successful Spanishness was repeated as a result of a comment by Albert Costa at a press conference after the match. When asked by an American journalist what Spaniards put in the water to make them so good at tennis, Costa answered: 'our secret is the food. Us Spaniards eat *jamón de jabugo*, *pata negra*'. *Jamón de Jabugo*, *pata negra* is a top class cured ham from Huelva, in Andalucía. Its excellence is so widely accepted that *pata negra* (that is, 'black leg', the colour of the pig after eating mainly acorns) has come to mean 'brilliant' in slang; but more importantly here, it is one of the culinary specialities that Spaniards have turned into an essential component not only of their diet but also of their national identity. This prompted headlines celebrating cured ham and Spanishness: 'The difference is that we eat cured ham' (*Abc*, 8 June 2002); 'The success of Jamón de Jabugo' (*El Mundo*, 8 June 2002); *La Vanguardia*, under its headline 'Spanish fiesta on clay' wrote 'a final with Jamón de Jabugo flavour' (9 June 2002).

The only exception was, rather unexpectedly, *Avui*, which resisted the temptation to call it a *Catalan* final, but also avoided establishing a link with previous Spanish victories in the French tennis open. In fact, *Avui* did not make as big a fuss of the victory of a Catalan player as one would have expected. Having identified the very Spanish cured ham as the reason for his victory (and not, for example, the more Catalan 'bread and tomato'), Costa did not leave *Avui* much leeway for its traditional arguments.

But not only that, at the same press conference, Costa said that that was a 'very great day for Spain. The football team has qualified and we have reached the final' (quoted in *Abc*, 8 June 2002). Despite Albert Costa's public identification with Spain as a whole, the column signed by Col-lectiu J.B. Boix in *Avui*, still wrote as an indictment to the Spanish press: 'We don't like the fact that Albert Costa is a Catalan player until he manages to win the Roland Garros Championship, then becoming a Spanish player' (23 June 2002). There is no evidence of such a change of heart in the Spanish press, and this comment should rather be regarded as proof that deeply entrenched discourses can sometimes be stronger than facts and can have a life of their own.

As a summary to this brief epilogue, it can be said that, in the coverage of the 2002 Football World Cup, *Avui* and very few columnists in other papers (mainly in *La Vanguardia* and *El País*) were exceptions to the general tendency to accept the use of the first-person plural to refer to the Spanish Football team, which was widely accepted now as a 'national' team worth supporting as a symbol of Spain. The game of criticism, rebuttal and rejection of the centralist unitarian discourse almost disappeared.

The Spanish final in the Roland Garros Championship also prompted a rhetoric of Spanish pride which leads us to believe that given the circumstances, Spanish society is keen, almost gasping, to get rid of the relationship between patriotism and Francoism. In that sense, the journalist Raúl del Pozo wrote in *El Mundo* an apology of the support of the national football team and an indictment against those who 'think that being in favour of Spain is typical of Francoists ... It is in football where the de-nationalization of the quaternarian Left is most evident'. That is, the 'quaternarian' (meaning 'Jurassic', 'primitive') Left has not yet realized that Franco's regime is over, that Spain is a different country, and therefore Spaniards can legitimately support their team without hang-ups.

Likewise, Ramón Irigoyen, in *El País*, allowed himself to ironize about Franco's influence on modern Spanish society in a article entitled 'Franco against Spain'. In reference to the 'curse' that had prevented Spain from winning the first match of a Football World Cup for the last fifty two years, he stated that 'the first culprit of this curse is – who else could it be? – Francisco Franco' (7 June 2002). This ironic urge to stop explaining Spanish modern reality in terms of its Francoist past is not just particular to the texts analysed here. One of the major aspirations of Spanish society is, indeed, its objective to 'forget' the past, and become a 'normal' and forward-looking country. Just like the rest of Europe. However, this aspiration to shed the past is not shared by everyone: as seen, for *Avui*, Spain is based on Francoist foundations and continues to be stuck in the Francoist past.

The debate concerning whether Spain is still Francoist or has overcome its undemocratic credentials is a crucial point in the analysis in the next chapter. As will be seen, after the first victory of the PP in 1996, this party 'proved' (according to *La Vanguardia* and CiU) that it had shed its Francoist traces. This 'transformation' allowed a pact with the Catalanists. After the second victory in 2000, the transformation of the PP and Spain as a whole was complete, or at least that was the reason given by *La Vanguardia* and CiU to continue their support for the PP in central government.

CHAPTER 3

CATALONIA: VICTIM AND REDEEMER OF SPAIN

1. Introduction

When the results of the 1996 elections failed to deliver an absolute majority for the PP and some kind of pact with the nationalist parties (in particular CiU) seemed the only possible way out of the ensuing impasse, the stakes for the two major players involved, as a number of the quotes reproduced below will show, were absolutely clear: failure to reach a workable agreement would have serious negative consequences for both parties, meaning that a pact of some kind *had to be achieved*. The problem this posed for both was that their previous political relationship had been based on high levels of mutual hostility. Each had, therefore, to find a way of persuading its supporters that the 'other' had changed in significant ways, thereby making an agreement possible.

This chapter will look at how that change was effected from the Catalanist side, in other words, the strategies used by the Catalanists to convince their grassroots supports that the PP was no longer the arch-enemy of yore, but a reformed character with whom an agreement was not only possible, but necessary. By concentrating on how this negotiation was carried out in *La Vanguardia*, historic mouthpiece of moderate Catalanism, the analysis will show how those managing this change of focus had consistent recourse – whether consciously or subconsciously (almost certainly the latter) – to a number of the structural characteristics of the traditional folk tale and indeed to a broader range of elements of narrative in general. A narrative is never, of course, a simple sequence of events (the 'fabula' of the Russian Formalists): it is a process whereby a series of values are contested, negotiated, defended or advanced using a series of mechanisms with which all readers (at least in western cultures) are extremely familiar.

The objectives of such a (fundamentally political) process were clear: two previously inimical narratives had to be merged into one, with the two former enemies eventually emerging as joint heroes in each other's narrative. As the analysis will show, the resources and structures of traditional narrative formats were fundamental to the writers of *La Vanguardia* in both the management and negotiation of such an outcome on behalf of CiU over a period of several weeks.

The Proppian perspective – What the Characters Do[1]

Propp's *Morphology of the Folktale* is a fundamental tool for this analysis. Reacting against the classification of folk tales according to their content, his analysis established that 'the structure or formal organization of a folkloristic text is described following the chronological order of the linear sequence of elements in the text' (introductory words of Alan Dundes, xi, Propp, 1984). Propp's model proposes that a fairy-tale can be reduced to thirty-one abstract functions, which are understood 'as an act of a character, defined from the point of view of its significance for the course of the action' (Propp, 1984: 21). These functions are distributed among seven *spheres of action* performable by varying characters giving way to an actantial framework constituted by: the villain, the donor, the helper, the sought-for person, the dispatcher, the hero and the false hero.

These functions are independent of the characters that carry them out or the shape they take – the nomenclature and attributes of the characters, the particularities of the setting, the varied form of injuries, obstacles or ordeals that a character might undergo are irrelevant to this formal model and only depend on the cultural and historical context of the particular fairy-tale (Propp, 1984: 88–89). Propp states that the sequence of these thirty-one functions is always the same in all folk tales and fairy-tales – that is, all of them have the same structure, although that does not imply that all tales must contain all thirty-one functions. The following is a presentation of the thirty-one functions and their description taken from Asa Berger (1997: 26):

	Function	Description
	initial situation	Members of family are introduced; hero is introduced (not considered a function).
1.	absentation	One of the members of the family absents him – or herself.
2.	interdiction	Interdiction addressed to hero (can be reversed).
3.	violation	Interdiction is violated.
4.	reconnaissance	Villain makes attempt to get information.
5.	delivery	Villain gets information about the victim.
6.	trickery	Villain tries to deceive victim.
7.	complicity	Victim is deceived.

8.	villainy	Villain causes harm to a member of the
	family;	
		or member of the family lacks something, desires something.
9.	mediation	Misfortune made known; hero is dispatched.
10	counteraction	Hero (seeker) agrees to counteraction.
11.	departure	Hero leaves home.
12.	1st donor function	Hero tested, receives magical agent or helper.
13.	hero's reaction	Hero reacts to agent or donor.
14.	receipt of agent	Hero acquires use of magical agent.
15.	spatial change	Hero led to object of search.
16.	struggle	Hero and victim join in direct combat.
17.	branding	Hero is branded.
18.	victory	Villain is defeated.
19.	liquidation	Initial misfortune or lack is liquidated.
20.	return	Hero returns.
21.	pursuit, chase	Hero is pursued.
22.	rescue	hero is rescued from pursuit.
23.	unrecognized arrival	Hero, unrecognized, arrives home or elsewhere.
24.	unfounded claims	False hero presents unfounded claims.
25.	difficult task	Difficult task is proposed to hero.
26.	solution	Task is resolved.
27.	recognition	Hero is recognized.
28.	exposure	False hero or villain is exposed.
29.	transfiguration	Hero is given a new appearance.
30.	punishment	Villain is punished.
31.	wedding	Hero is married, ascends the throne.

A brief summary (offered by Frederic Jameson) of the functions established by Propp is worth mentioning here. The victim undergoes injury or the lack of some important object:

> The hero, if he is not himself personally involved, is sent for, at which point two key events take place. He meets the donor ... who after testing him for the appropriate reaction ... supplies him with a magical agent ... which enables him to pass victoriously through his ordeal. Then ... he meets the villain, engaging him in

decisive combat ... There is an alternate track [to the combat with the villain] in which the hero finds himself before a series of tasks or labors which, with the help of his agent, he is ultimately able to solve properly ... the latter part of the tale is little more than a series of retarding devices: the pursuit of the hero on his way home, the possible intrusion of a false hero, the unmasking of the latter, with the ultimate transfiguration, marriage and/or coronation of the hero himself (Jameson, 1974: 65–66).

Propp's apparatus can be applied to cultural fields beyond fairy-tales. At times, as Fiske has shown in his application of the model to television drama, 'the conformity is astonishing in its precision' (Fiske, 1987: 137); other times some modifications, repetition or degrees of emphasis of functions and character roles must be taken into account (*ibid*: 137–138). In the narrative analysed here the traditional pattern was at times followed and at times modified, according to the political interests of *La Vanguardia*/CiU. A brief introduction to the events that took place between the electoral campaign before the 1996 elections and the final pact between the PP and CiU, and how they were constructed in a narrative form by *La Vanguardia* (fully analysed in this chapter) will help clarify the application of Propp's model and the deviations to such a model.

Summary of Events

Throughout the campaign leading up to the general elections of 3 March 1996 opinion polls swung from giving the right-wing party Partido Popular (PP) less than a majority of seats to granting them an overall majority. The political stance of the Catalanist coalition Convergència i Unió (CiU) was affected by the results of the opinion polls and they varied their electoral slogans according to them: if at the beginning they went for a conciliatory motto *serem clau* ('we will be key') that reflected their intention to maintain the pivotal role that they had enjoyed while in the agreement with the PSOE, the threat of an overall majority made them adopt a more confrontational stance reflected in the slogan *plantarem cara* ('we will stand up to them').

As noted previously, the actual results gave the PP 156 parliamentary seats out of a total of 350 seats – that is, a substantial shortfall from the expected and hoped-for overall majority. This meant that, in order to form a government, the PP would have to look for support elsewhere. From the very beginning the Catalan nationalists of Convergència i Unió were the best-placed candidates. While cooperation between PSOE and CiU in the period between 1993 to 1996 had been relatively effective, a pact or any sort of alliance with the PP was much more difficult. As seen in detail in chapter 1 the PP had been accused by CiU of anti-Catalanism as a result of its strategy of attack against the PSOE with regard to the latter's 'dependence' on the Catalanists; for accusing CiU of political and economic blackmail; and for the campaign against the linguistic policy of the Generalitat (supported by a majority in the Catalan Parliament). Moreover, the PP was accused by CiU of lacking in some of the most cherished values of Catalanism: the democratic credibility (they were deemed the heirs of Franco) and European spirit; and, above all, were accused of a clear reluctance to accept the idea of a plurinational Spain.

In such an uncertain juncture, with the possibility of a negotiation between two supposedly radically opposed parties, a way out of the stalemate would have been to ask for new elections which would clarify the situation. The Catalan nationalists rejected this out of hand. It should be remembered that the possibility of holding new elections entailed the risk of losing the unexpectedly good results obtained by CiU (16 seats – only one less than in the previous election). If the results had not been as good and the prospects of intervening in central government had not been so clear, there might have been a greater incentive for the Catalan nationalists to call for a new election. The other possibility put forward by the nationalists was the re-creation of the cooperative 'spirit of the transition to democracy' in which none of the parties would reject a right-wing government. CiU's idea was to have the PSOE abstain in the vote of confidence. However, given that the PSOE was not prepared to abstain, CiU had to begin a change of discourse.

It has to be said that the negotiations between Aznar and Pujol were long and, very importantly, extremely secretive. It took fifty-three days to reach an agreement, including seventeen hours of secret meetings between the two leaders. At one point Pujol stated that 'the healthy thing to do is for us not to make too many statements so that we can negotiate with calm and tranquility' (*La Vanguardia* 21 March). What the readers of *La Vanguardia* received was – as always – a narrative interpretation of what was going on. At times commentators and editors of *La Vanguardia* seemed to be aware of the narrative nature of their interpretations of the events. In that sense, the newspaper, once the way towards the pact had been paved, wrote in its editorial with the benefit of hindsight: 'today everyone is aware that the last acts of a play of which everyone knows the resolution, are being performed' (17 April).

The first result of this secretive political negotiation was made public on 18 March after the first meeting between José María Aznar and Jordi Pujol in Madrid where Aznar publicly accepted some of the most important premises of moderate Catalanism regarding Spain and the role of Catalonia within the State. The PP accepted, amongst other measures, a new system of funding of the Autonomous Communities with the granting of their right to manage 30% of tax revenue; compulsory military service was scrapped; the centralist figure of the 'gobernador civil' (the representative of Central Government in each province) was also eliminated; and the Generalitat obtained the powers to manage the two main Catalan ports of Barcelona and Tarragona.

The actual signing of the pact took place on 28 April 1996 in Barcelona (and not in Madrid!), which was regarded as a victory for the Catalanists. The vote of investiture in the Central Parliament was on 4 May.

Summary of the Narrative Encoding of the Events[2]

The fierceness of the attacks of the PP on CiU during the previous parliamentary term had been so intense that the depiction of the relationship between the two parties carried out by *La Vanguardia* was more along the lines of enmity than political opposition. The general picture as presented by *La Vanguardia* was that before the elections the PP had been using a dangerous and unjust strategy consisting of an anti-CiU, anti-Catalanist and anti-Catalan stance directed towards gaining political power at any cost. The actions of the PP were constructed along the lines of 'acts of villainy' – to use Propps's terms (1984: 31) – that left the bond between the players 'burnt out' (José María Brunet, political editor of *La Vanguardia*, 14 March). Not surprisingly, in the aftermath of the elections the prospects of a pact/alliance/agreement with the PP were presented as virtually non-existent. The first encounter of these two political 'enemies' was often metaphorically encoded as a competition. For instance: two contenders playing a game of chess (*La Vanguardia,* 7 March) or, more dramatically, two racing drivers about to have a head-on collision (Juan Tàpia, editor of *La Vanguardia*, 8 March). In the situation prior to and immediately after the elections there were (according to this interpretation) two main characters: the Catalan Hero (CiU, whose heroic status will be developed below) and the Villain (the PP). The electoral slogan 'we will stand up to them' can be rightly understood as a sort of 'interdiction' (function 2) to negotiating with the PP.

However, after the PSOE's refusal to abstain in the vote of confidence and the failure of the revival of the 'spirit of the transition', the aftermath of the general election started to be constructed as a point of temporal segmentation in the relationship between the PP and CiU, a turning point that would establish a 'before' and an 'after'. For both Catalanist politicians and most columnists in *La Vanguardia*, the result of the election was read now as a momentous point in the history of Spain on the grounds that it was the first time that a Spanish right-wing party had won a general election since Franco's death. Unión de Centro Democrático, the first party elected to government after Franco's death, was, at least nominally, a centre party. This moment was also being constructed as marking the opportunity, and even the necessity, for a rapprochement between the Spanish Right and the peripheral nationalists. In order to justify such an unexpected and politically delicate pact, the process would have to be endowed with all the pomp and ceremony of a historical event that would entail not only an endorsement of the new government's policy in the opening session of the parliament, but also throughout the whole four-year parliamentary term and beyond, in the construction of the grandiosely called 'Spanish State of the XXI century'.

This rapprochement of CiU towards the PP involved a radical change in their narrative, and at this point functions number 8 (villainy, lack) and 9 (mediation) were pivotal: although the villain kept on carrying out 'acts of villainy', at the same time the hero acknowledged a lack (the absence of a government) in the community and undertook to resolve it. Therefore, in the new narrative the Catalan hero was not 'dispatched' (function 9) to 'join in direct combat with the villain' (function 16) but to negotiate with the former enemy.

Consequently, the relationship between the characters would go now from competition to exchange and communication. In order to avoid any kind of agreement being interpreted as a 'violation' of an interdiction (function 3), or as complicity with the villain (functions 6 and 7), the mediation of the Catalan hero had to be heavily qualified. The idea was that in order for the PP to be able to receive the necessary votes they would have to fulfill certain conditions within the narrative. These conditions were nothing less than the acceptance of the most cherished premises of Catalan nationalism: in other words, they would have to be seen to accept the Catalanist discourse. This meant that in the negotiation not only parliamentary votes but, more importantly, ideological values would be involved.

The fulfillment of these conditions was given in the form of a test (first part of function 12: the potential hero is tested), an ordeal whereby the enemy would have to prove that it had acquired competence for political power. That is, the PP had to prove something to CiU, its grassroots and Catalonia, a situation which put José María Aznar's party in a position of being examined.

In order to avoid accusations from the Catalanist grassroots of 'complicity' with the PP, there was a need to stress the uneven distribution of competence among the characters. Using the head-on collision metaphor mentioned above, the regular columnist of *La Vanguardia* Martí Gómez said:

> everyone is certain that [Pujol] will be able to dodge the head-on collision, but it is extremely doubtful that Aznar will come through unscathed: most probably, they say, he will skid and will end up at the bottom of a precipice and be forced to give things away (Martí Gómez, *La Vanguardia,* 7 March).

Furthermore, in this ordeal, and in keeping with the uneven distribution of competence, CiU presented itself as keeping the upper hand, controlling the situation according to its needs: 'we will take the decision when it suits us, not Mr. Aznar or González' (*La Vanguardia*, 11 March), Pujol was reported as saying, showing control over the pace and the timetable of the negotiations. This situation constructed a powerless PP giving way to the demands of CiU. In that sense *La Vanguardia* wrote in one of its editorials when the pact was about to be signed: 'The PP could not help but give in to the wishes of CiU if they wanted Aznar to count on the votes of the nationalists' (26 April). This control over the situation did not even spare the place of the official signing of the pact, with all its symbolic connotations. In a report of *La Vanguardia* the securing of this final victory was announced: 'in the end, Pujol got his way, and this evening the formal act of the signing of the agreement might take place ... in Barcelona' (28 April) – that is, not in Madrid.

According to the logic of the traditional folk tale, the character that overcomes a test is the hero. In this particular narrative, there was a complication: the character subjected to the test was the former villain. The situation, therefore, implied that there existed the possibility for the former enemy to become a hero. The result of the test (function 13) was interpreted by the commentators of *La Vanguardia* in two opposite ways:

- As positive. This interpretation of the result of the test celebrated the final rapprochement of the two former enemies and the Spanish Right's acceptance and recognition of the values of the Catalanists and their legitimate role in Spanish politics. This 'happy ending' implied two recognitions (function 27). Firstly, the new hero (the PP) was publicly recognized. Secondly, the Catalan hero was also recognized by those who previously regarded the Catalanists and Catalonia as villains, as foes of Spain. A very important difference between both recognitions should be taken into account: the recognition of the Partido Popular was considered as the result of a transformation, whereas the recognition of Catalonia was regarded as a long-overdue act of justice. This double recognition was presented as the event that would finally allow the final *encaix*, the political and administrative fitting in of Catalonia within a regenerated and emergent Spain. The subsequent function would be the signing of the pact, which would be presented as a 'wedding' (function 31).

- As negative (function 13). This interpretation of the result of the test involved a whole show of reservations, incredulity and even negation of the supposed transformation of the PP. Such a rendering of events followed the long-standing interpretations of an apparently unavoidably immovable relationship between Catalonia and the rest of Spain; and even more, the impossibility of the regeneration of Spain (more in line with the political stance of *Avui*, as seen in the previous chapter).

An even more radical interpretation of the whole sequence of events would reduce the whole of the narrative to an act of trickery on the part of the villain (function 6) together with the complicity of the Catalan hero in its own 'deceit' (function 7).

2. The Catalanist Differential Narrative

Sequential Segmentation

This analysis will concentrate on the process of potential transformation of the identity of the PP (as representative of the conservative, Eternal Spain) expressed in a sequence of conjunctions and disjunctions with certain values. The scope of the narrative can be segmented into three main moments separated by a turning point:

a) initial confrontation

b) external event constituting a turning point plus preparation for the contract

c) the contract.

The preparation for the contract included a transformation whereby Eternal Spain had to renounce its former values and, at the same time, acquire others it lacked. Whether the transformation of PP/Eternal Spain was real or false would become a matter of debate also dealt with in this study. However, for the sake of clarity, I will consider the success story – i.e. the one which regards the change as 'real' – as the basis of the analysis. According to this interpretation, the sequences before and after the contract constituted two contrasting set-ups both in their actantial organization and in the characterization and value-systems of the subjects involved.

Actorial Organization

Plantarem cara ('we will stand up to them') was one of the slogans used by the Catalan nationalists in the run up to the elections. It epitomized not only the political stance of the CiU facing the possibility of a right-wing government, but also the relationship between Catalonia and what the PP supposedly represented (both traditionally and at that particular time): that part of Spain historically related to the values of the Francoist past, centralism and anti-Catalanism.

The three main actors of this narrative are PP, PSOE and CiU. The next extract will help illustrate and elaborate on the nature of these characters as constructed by the moderate Catalanist discourse of *La Vanguardia* in 1996. The columnist Baltasar Porcel, in an article significantly entitled 'Style and Values', commented on the difference between Catalonia and the rest of Spain by quoting an opinion to which he subscribed: 'In Catalonia ... there are certain problems ... but people want to sort them out carefully, and not by shouting and fighting'. And then he continued:

> This is what the Spanish PP does not understand and the Catalan PP refused to understand. In order to visualize the difference we will have to go back to the Aznarist night of 3 March, with their flags, hurrahs and insults that, in Catalonia, struck fear into vast numbers of television viewers of all ideologies. Let's not dramatize, but the style of that Carpetovetonic[3] citizenship is rough, alien to the way in which the vast majority of people in Catalonia understand things, living-together[4], happiness (*La Vanguardia*, 14 March).

The first inference to be drawn from this is the idea of the existence of at least two Spains, of which only one is mentioned: 'the Carpetovetonic Spanish citizenship', composed of the supporters of PP. This group is clearly related to Francoism by the reference to 'their flags', meaning not only Spanish flags (which in itself turns them into Spanish nationalists), but also the Francoist Pre-Constitutional flags that some people were waving on election night. Conversely, there is the implication of the existence of shared values across the board in Catalonia ('viewers of all ideologies').

The second inference that can be drawn following Roland Barthes (1972: 138) is that in order to create the idea of Catalan homogeneity all the elements that the prevailing ideology considers alien are excluded. That is the implication of the supposed refusal of the Catalan PP to sort out the problems without 'shouting and fighting': the Spanish PP does not understand because it is alien to Catalan values; the Catalan PP (naturally in possession of such values through being Catalan) consciously refuses to understand – that is, it is a thought-through refusal to accept something that is part of their value system.

This is not at all an isolated element in the discourse of a particular writer (here I am interested not in the texts in their difference but in the common features that build up the narrative). This tendency towards the creation of a homogeneous society is part and parcel of the discourse discussed here. In the political arena, the PP is generally presented as 'a reality alien to Catalan society that has had to create new and somewhat artificial leaders', as Miquel Serrallès, editor of the magazine

Debat Nacionalista puts it. Serrallès also concedes that 'whether we like it or not, PSC–PSOE is an important part of the Catalan social body' (*La Vanguardia*, 14 March) – PSC–PSOE being, incidentally, the most voted-for party in the March '96 general elections in Catalonia obtaining 19 of the 46 seats.

Taking these extracts as representative of a widespread tendency, it can be stated that within the ideological parameters of this narrative discourse, its actorial structure can be reduced to three main actors:

> a) CiU as representatives of Catalonia;
>
> b) one sector of Spain sensitive to Catalanist proposals about the conception of the State (represented by PSOE); and
>
> c) another sector of Spain stuck with more centralist and 'old-fashioned' ideas denominated by Eternal Spain and represented by the Partido Popular.

The Hero, the Villain, the Donor and their Narrative Programmes

According to moderate Catalanist discourse, one of the objectives of Catalonia is to become a normalized active part of the Spanish State, which would imply: a) the definite integration of Catalonia within Spain; b) intervention in its affairs, and c) at the same time, the full recognition of Catalan national rights and maximum degree of autonomy. On the other hand (still according to the moderate Catalanist discourse) the objective of Eternal Spain is the maintenance and strengthening of the centralist conception of the Spanish State (which implies an elimination of the values and national rights of Catalonia). In this discourse, Eternal Spain and Catalonia compete against each other for possession of the same object: and this object is none other than Spain. This 'object of desire' should be understood, of course, as an idea or a conception of Spain. And the 'possession' of Spain should be understood as imposing the hegemony of a view of the country not only in terms of political legality but also in terms of public opinion, which in many respects is where the real power lies.

This confrontation was organized around two correlative axes that ran in opposite directions to each other. In narrative semiotics, they are called *parallel programmes*. The Catalanist programme constituted the *fundamental programme* since it is from this perspective that the analysis is carried out. This programme was impeded or fought against by its *parallel* or *anti-programme*, that of the PP (as constructed, that is, by the Catalanist discourse). In the particular case I am concerned with here, the PP's anti-programme is graphically illustrated by Pi as the 'many obstacles, many difficulties in the application of the instruments that can turn into a reality what Jordi Pujol calls the will to be' of Catalonia, that is, 'the preservation of her characteristic features in culture, law, language and economy' (Pi and Pujol, 1996: 22). It is, in short, the obstacles standing in the way of the integration of the Catalanist vision of Catalonia, always regarded as 'within the Spanish reality' (Pi and Pujol, 1996: 29). It needs to be pointed out here that what CiU understands as PP's narrative is just another construction of the Partido Popular's ideology and attitude towards Catalonia and Spain.

The Hero and the Villain

The subject of the fundamental programme is the hero. In the first confrontational stage of the narrative CiU/Catalonia fulfilled the role of the victim–hero, that is, of the one who suffers the actions of the villain in Propp's definition (1984: 50). From the perspective of the fundamental programme, the PP/Eternal Spain was in turn constructed as the foe or enemy (the PP is the 'the natural enemy' said *La Vanguardia*, 14 March). And the status of the villainous PP was constructed along Proppian lines in three main ways:

a) As the one that causes a lack (Propp, 1984: 34). The PP at the time of the analysis was presented as the direct descendants of the Franco regime. The nationalist leader Joaquima Alemany directly related the acts of the Franco regime to the PP's politics: 'how can an agreement be reached with a party ... which has not in the slightest helped to recover our institutions, our culture, and our language and which calls "particularities" what are signs of identity' (*La Vanguardia*, 10 March); 'particularities' being the way Franco's regime dealt with the signs of Catalan and other peripheral identities. The PP was accused of attempting to destroy two of the most precious and widely accepted attributes of Catalonia: consensus and the ideal of *convivència* (as Miquel Serrallès, put it in *La Vanguardia*, 14 March).

b) Villainies were also constructed as part of an all-out war (Propp, 1984: 34). In this sense, Josep M. Sòria, deputy director of information of *La*

Vanguardia, talked of 'the aggressive attitude of the PP and its media spokespersons during the last three years, [which] make the way towards consensus really difficult' (7 March). Quoting a nationalist leader he continued: 'it has been a catastrophic, disastrous opposition. It's been really bad. An opposition based on destruction and permanent insult' (*ibid*).

The Donor

In the run-up to the general election and all the way until the pact was secured, the Spanish Left, and the Socialists in particular, were regarded as more understanding of the Catalanist movement, thereby performing the role of the donor: 'The Left has been historically more given to assuming this approach. The distance covered in the last years proves it, despite the mistakes made' said the regular columnist of *La Vanguardia*, López-Burniol (18 February). The importance given to the role of the PSOE as donor is quite remarkable, bearing in mind that the most pro-federalist of all-Spanish parties is not PSOE but Izquierda Unida (IU, in fact a left-wing coalition). However, their presentation as helpers was avoided for two main reasons: first of all, despite its support for self-determination, IU is a left-wing grouping whose economic and social stances do not enjoy much popularity among the Catalanist middle classes; secondly, IU was accused in the previous parliamentary term of collaboration with the 'anti-Catalanist' PP in its demolition of the PSOE and their then political partners, CiU.

Electoral Aftermath: Continued Confrontation

In the PP and its co-attendant media, since their objective almost immediately after the election was to reach an agreement with the nationalists, there was an instantaneous change in the strategy of confrontation towards CiU. The conservative Madrid newspaper *Abc,* a continuous supporter of the PP, justified the prospective pact in terms of normality on the grounds of the common ideology of the two parties when it suggested that 'the understanding, the agreement, the pact between the two parties with a common ideology and belonging to the same International ... is a return to normality' (*Abc*, 6 March). The concrete reasons attributed to the PP for the suitability of the pact were 'the basic similarities in the [political] programmes of the PP [and] CiU on the European framework, on economic policies' and, more surprisingly, 'on the Autonomies' (quoted by *La Vanguardia*, 7 March). In fact the quick reaction of *Abc* should not be seen as something completely unexpected since, just after the European Elections in 12

June 1994, which gave a clear victory to the PP, this party started to open up to the nationalists (the PNV and CiU in particular) with the aim of the 'normalization of their relationship' (*Abc*, 23 June 1994). As far as CiU was concerned the main agent of these talks was Duran i Lleida, leader of Unió Democràtica – one of the member-parties of the coalition CiU, who as *Abc* remarked was 'one of the leaders who was most keen to start a dialogue with the PP' (*ibid*).

However, CiU's first reactions to the electoral results were characterized by a continuation of the confrontational attitude, that is, of a refusal of any kind of pact with the enemy. In the early stages the Catalan nationalist leader Xabier Trias viewed a vote for the formation of a PP government as 'a remote option' (*La Vanguardia*, 7 March); and a pact with the PP as 'very difficult' or even 'impossible' (*La Vanguardia*, 8 March) because 'CiU is, in principle against the PP' (*La Vanguardia* 7 March) and because, as the Catalanist leader Joaquim Molins put it, 'the PP has turned the Catalan nationalists into a permanent target of tense criticism denying some of the principles that CiU regards as essential' (*La Vanguardia*, 8 March).

The reaction of the PP politicians and grassroots – some of whom shouted 'Pujol, enano, habla castellano' [Pujol, you dwarf, speak Castilian] in the election night – to the result of the elections was one of the episodes most commented upon, and was generally presented as living proof of the negative set of values that characterized the PP within the Catalanist narrative. The following passage will suffice to illustrate this point:

> They had taken the flag of Spain onto the streets ... And they carried the flag in procession as if it were the uncorrupted arm of Saint Teresa; as if they were in the Santiago Bernabéu Stadium and at that very moment Marcelino had just scored the goal that gave us the victory against Russia in the European Championship.
>
> They took out the flag, the flag of all Spaniards in order to celebrate their victory ... it was like an image taken from the film libraries, of the most worn-out celluloid, of a remote yesteryear... They used the flag as a throwing weapon, as an element of discord, as if it were entirely theirs (Manuel Trallero, *La Vanguardia* 10 March).

Although I do not intend to carry out a detailed analysis of the extract, some points should be highlighted. The title from which this extract is taken is 'Banderas al viento' ('Flags in the Wind'), the second line of the 'Montañas Nevadas', one of the most representative of Francoist anthems. With this reference, the author hints at the intention of the whole article: the relationship between the victorious PP and Francoism; hence the comparison of the scene with an image 'taken out of the film libraries, of the most worn-out celluloid, of a remote yesteryear'; or with the nationalist euphoria after the victory of the Spanish national team over the Soviet Union back in the sixties (an episode of the sporting and political history of Spain which is still vividly remembered by Catalan journalists, as seen in the previous chapter). The allusion to the tacky sacredness with which the Right supposedly regards the Spanish nation, is exemplified by the comparison of the Spanish flag with the uncorrupted arm of the Castilian Saint Teresa of Ávila (converted by Spanish National Catholicism – the religious ideology of the Franco regime – into an essential Spanish icon whose uncorrupted limb was in the personal possession of Franco until his death). Lastly, the appropriation of the flag 'of all the Spaniards' in order to celebrate 'their' victory is for the author a sign of the exclusivist nature of Spanish right-wing nationalism and an index of its tendency to sow discord among all Spaniards.

3. Turning Point and Preparation for the Test

Despite the first moments of confrontation and out-of-hand rejection of the pact, the static tension between CiU and PP soon started to lose momentum. In four of the 17 Autonomous Communities the nationalist/regionalist parties maintained or increased their electoral support: PNV and Coalición Canaria maintained their share of the vote; ETA's political wing Herri Batasuna retained its parliamentary seats; the Galician nationalists of Bloque Nacionalista Galego gained 2 seats. However, the Catalan nationalists of CiU suffered some damage, losing one seat. Be that as it may, this minor defeat did not prevent CiU from turning into the clearest candidate for some kind of pact or coalition with PP. From then on, the Catalanist coalition had to justify the prospective pact in a way that would not be at odds with the traditional discourse of moderate Catalanism.

However, the first strategy of CiU was to demand the support of the other parties in the formation of the government. Accordingly, from *La Vanguardia*, the regular columnist Oriol Pi de Cabanyes demanded a 'second transition'– reviving that period of consensus of all the democratic parties for the construction of the new Constitutional State (*La Vanguardia*, 7 March).[5] Or, as *La Vanguardia* put it, the Catalan nationalists 'do not rule out a stable pact and are looking for one-off agreements involving other parties to guarantee the investiture of Aznar and avoid new elections' (8 March). This move implied a demand to the PSOE for an abstention in the Vote of Confidence, which would have been enough for the formation of a Government.

However, the PSOE were adamant they would vote against the PP. This situation (rather than the electoral results themselves) was the external event that represented a breach in the continuity of a confrontational situation and would change the relationship between the CiU and PP. At that moment CiU found itself obliged to start a change of discourse and a rapprochement towards the political 'villain'. On 8 March *La Vanguardia* informed in an approving tone that the initial 'monolithic position' had been abandoned in favour of a new more pragmatic one since 'the passage of time is breaking down maximalist positions'. On 8 March, the newspaper editor Juan Tàpia, although admitting the attitude of the PP during the previous term made it difficult for the Catalan voters to accept a pact with the PP, warned his readers that 'only the pact between PP and CiU ... would secure a government for the new term' (8 March). The same editor urged the nationalists, reproducing the words uttered by Jordi Pujol, not 'to slam the door' on the PP (*La Vanguardia*, 10 March). As will be seen below, this move towards the 'enemy' would end up being constructed as necessary and even obligatory for CiU, Catalonia and the whole of Spain.

Lack and Mediation

The new strategy would be governed by the other electoral slogan brandished during the run-up to the election: 'serem clau' ('we will be key'). As *La Vanguardia* stated in its report on the first General Meeting of Convergència Democràtica de Catalunya, as early as 7 March 'there were no maximalist voices favouring the slogan 'we will confront them' to the other one ... 'we will be key''. It was becoming clear that for the Catalanist politicians the pact was not a remote possibility anymore. And in clear support of such a political change, Martí Gómez stated in one of his regular columns in *La Vanguardia* that 'Catalonia has been and will keep on being key in the future of Spain for a long time' (7 March).

La Vanguardia was attempting a justification of the change in the relationship between the PP–Eternal Spain and CiU–Catalonia on the basis of the historical key role played by Catalanists in Spanish politics. This change demanded that the Catalan hero be turned from hero–victim which suffered at the hands of the PP, to hero–donor whose task was now the resolution of a lack in the country – the political stability and governability of the State. Just like in folk tales, 'the initial desire' of the hero, in this case the Catalan hero, was:

> based upon the verification of a lack ... [and] the raison d'être of the subject is precisely the liquidation of such lack, carried out by means of the performing hero ... and followed by a gift, that is, the transference of the ... Object–Value to the society where this lack had made itself evident (Greimas, 1980: 128).

This is a lack that, according to the interpretation of the events carried out by *La Vanguardia* and the Catalanist politicians themselves, the Catalan hero took upon itself to overcome. In other words, the hero was prepared to mediate. The function of mediation has major consequences for a narrative. Firstly, as Propp points out, this function 'brings the hero into the tale' (1984: 36). In the narrative analysed here, the Catalan hero had never been *out* of the tale – rather, the alteration of the narrative lay in the nature of the character: as noted above, from being a victim–hero, there was now a move towards being an active character in the new juncture. In Greimasian terms it meant a qualitative transformation of the Catalan character from constituting a *subject of being* into a *subject of doing*. From being a mere repository of values attributed to it or subtracted from it, CiU–Catalonia moved on to being the executor of a narrative programme, which is tantamount to saying that it became in control of the situation, perfectly described by Oriol Pi de Cabanyes when he wrote in one of his regular opinion columns, with the benefit of hindsight, '[us Catalans] can now vent our opinions' (*La Vanguardia*, 21 March).

Secondly, the construction of the role of CiU as a mediator introduced a further change in the kind of relationship between with the PP: from competition or struggle, the relationship had to metamorphose into one of potential contract. The possibility of an agreement had a crucial effect: from being subject and anti-subject, CiU and the PP became potential giver or donor and receiver, respectively. Contract is the dominant function in the interaction of characters in a society. This type of relation takes the form of an exchange of objects according to the following narrative scheme: Subject 1 and Subject 2 have certain objects they are willing to get rid of in exchange for other objects that the other subject has. This is the way in which a coalition pact between two parties should be understood: as a give-and-take until a final compromise is reached.

However, the fact that the lack to be liquidated by the Catalan hero was that of the former enemy, established the particularity of this narrative construction of the negotiations. Maybe it is opportune to remember again that the 'irreconcilable' PP and CiU (Lluís Foix, deputy editor of *La Vanguardia*, 19 March) were complete antagonists in the initial stages of their relationship. A pact with PP would be 'against nature' said Mr. Serrallès (*La Vanguardia*, 14 March). Therefore, for the grass roots any trace of compromise would have meant a sell-out of CiU's political premises regarding the structure of the Spanish State. It would have been perceived as a step backwards in what Catalonia had already gained in terms of national rights after the transition to the democratic State.

Therefore, presenting CiU and PP as two subjects negotiating on an equal footing was out of the question. As a result of this, the process towards an agreement had to be constructed still at this stage as following the structure of confrontation, but now falling into the mythical scheme of the test. The conditions that, according to the Catalanists and *La Vanguardia*, the PP had to comply with will be dealt with in more detail in section entitled 'The Test'.

The Catalan Hero Prepares to Leave Home

In many narratives, mediation might entail that the hero is first allowed to leave home (Propp: 36–37). The first meeting of Convergència Democràtica after the elections (6 March) inaugurated the sequence of preparation for the granting of permission to the leader of CiU to start negotiations. Around that time, the obligations that the PP had to comply with were laid out with the assistance of editors and regular columnists of *La Vanguardia* (dealt with in the next section). Self-imposed obligations that CiU would have to fulfil (dealt with later in this section) were also established then.

The difficult situation of the CiU politicians, facing a pact with the political enemy, was illustrated by *La Vanguardia* in one of its headlines: 'Pujol will have to stand up to his party so that they don't veto a pact with the PP' (10 March); in other words, the hero would have to ask for permission. This would be presented as a difficult task seen by critics as 'a well thought-out excuse to justify what is unjustifiable' (Miquel Serrallès, *La Vanguardia*, 14 March). The meeting was intended to allay reservations expressed in questions such as the following: 'How would the voters understand a pact with Spanish nationalism? ... This would be a pact against nature' (*ibid*). At the end of the day, as the editor of *La Vanguardia* stated, since 1993 'PP and CiU have been two conflicting groups in permanent confrontation during the last term of office ... and the association – which many Catalan voters make – of the PP with anti-Catalanism makes the formula very difficult' (Juan Tàpia, *La Vanguardia,* 8 March). Therefore, this test was, as one nationalist leader put it, with the benefit of hindsight, as a strategy to allow the 'grass roots to assimilate the eventual possibility of an agreement, so that CiU can become the 'key' to the governability [of the State]' (*La Vanguardia*, 22 March).

Given the difficulty, this rapprochement towards the enemy had to be carefully constructed, always making sure that CiU–Catalonia was not depicted as approaching PP–Eternal Spain, but vice versa. All along CiU was seen as exerting her free will, her sovereignty and her freedom of movement. This point was put forward by Pujol when he threatened to 'fall back inside, towards Catalonia' if the Socialists (now most probably becoming the opposition) decided to orchestrate yet 'another campaign against Catalonia like the one performed by the PP' in the previous term of office (*La Vanguardia*, 11 March).

Qualifying the Will to Mediate

In this section I will introduce the process of construction of the Catalan Subject for future action. In the previous section it has been emphasized that the action of Catalonia was characterized as sovereign. In that sense, the conditions (or terms of contract) under which future action would be carried out had to be seen as self-imposed or, at least, not contradictory to the normal line of action of the character. Only when those conditions had been agreed upon, would the hero be given permission to leave home and become the future donor of the former foe. So, which were the conditions that made it justifiable for Catalonia to approach the Eternal Spain of the PP?:

a) The people's will as expressed in the electoral results. For the political editor of the paper, J.M. Brunet, the PP was obliged to organize an agreement with the Catalan nationalists since 'the result of the election confirms support for a certain conception of Spain that asserts its plurality' (*La Vanguardia*, 10 March). As seen above, this interpretation of the results might have been true for other peripheral nationalist parties, but certainly not for CiU, which indeed lost one MP.

A further justification of CiU's involvement in the pact was the interpretation of the electoral results as a historical turning point, since a right-wing party had won the elections for the first time since Franco's death. This immediately sparked off the interpretation of this event as a potential moment of encounter of an all-Spanish right-wing party and nationalist parties, and, by implication, the Right's acceptance of the role of peripheral nationalist ideology in Spanish politics. In that sense, this potential historical encounter was regarded by *La Vanguardia*, in its editorial comment, as opening a new era for Catalonia (8 March). And Martí Gómez took care to remind his readers that an agreement with all-Spanish parties was not contradictory with Catalonia's history: 'Catalonia has been and will keep on being key in the future of Spain for a long time' (*La Vanguardia*, 7 March).

Equally importantly, the maintenance or increase in support for peripheral parties (although not for CiU), triggered the idea of the end of the prevailing and well-established grand narrative of 'the Two Spains' and its underlying implication that the country as a whole is divided into binary groups (Left and Right, modern and backward, etc). This is an ideological split that remains indifferent to pluralistic, differential or peripheral ways of conceiving Spain without referring to the centre:

> The simple, one-dimensional and monolithic Spain has lost. The victory has been for a new project for the future that will not come true without the gathering of Catalans, Basques, Galicians or Canarians, aware of their difference. And if none of the Spains ... has pulled it off, that is because plurality is the new thing (*La Vanguardia*, 8 March).

If the results of the elections supposedly produced a historical 'opportunity' for changing the State (Oriol Pi de Cabanyes, *La Vanguardia*, 7 March), the new situation, as the regular columnist of *La Vanguardia*, J.M. Sòria stated, also 'will force the Right to accept that Spain, at last, is a plurinational and plurilingual reality' (*La Vanguardia*, 7 March), which has been an essential claim of Catalanism for a long time.

b) Political duty. The historical participation of Catalonia in the rest of Spain was justified mainly by political duty towards the State. This political duty was presented as driven by 'reason', 'responsibility', and 'the need for involvement in Spanish politics', all part and parcel of Catalan self-depiction.

- <u>Reason</u>. One of the stormiest meetings of CiU after the elections (10 March) was presented as 'seven hours of catharsis' (*La Vanguardia*, 11 March), that is, as a sort of purge of strong emotions, fears, tensions or unhappy memories by talking about them openly and expressing them. This moment of reflection took the form of a triumph of reason over emotions, which is in itself in line with the idea of the proverbial Catalan *seny*.

- In a second image used by *La Vanguardia*, the 10 March meeting was described as 'a debate between brain and heart' (11 March). This divide between what CiU really wanted and felt (the heart) and the obligations that reason imposed (the brain), were also explained by the editorial comment of the newspaper. It constructed an image of CiU as a party divided between its *desire* – not to reach an agreement with a party that the electorate regards 'as the bête-noire of their national assertion' – and its rational *obligation* – 'what reason is demanding' is 'to contribute to the governability of the State at a decisive moment on its way towards political and economic convergence with Maastricht Europe' (*La Vanguardia*, 11 March).

It should be added here that, after the pact was secured, *La Vanguardia*, in its editorial, stated that the agreement was 'the only politically *rational* way out' (*La Vanguardia*, 28 April, my italics).

<u>Responsibility</u>. As *La Vanguardia* put it, it would be Jordi Pujol himself who would have to tip the balance towards reason by appealing to the 'need to keep all doors open to hypothetical agreements', and by calling on 'the responsibility of the grass roots' (*La Vanguardia*, 10 March). *La Vanguardia* expressed Pujol's plans as follows: 'he will appeal to the responsibility of the grass roots about the need not to block any exploratory avenues with the PP' (10 March). Again, this justifying sense of responsibility was reinforced with a reminder of the long-standing and non-contradictory contributing attitude of CiU, which 'has always had a great sense of responsibility towards the governability both of Catalonia and Spain, where they have collaborated in government without giving up their commitment to their own programme, to their electorate and to Catalonia' (Joaquima Alemany, CiU leader, *La Vanguardia*, 10 March).

Through the call to responsibility the party was invested with a must, an obligation that was given priority over desire. This moved CiU/Catalonia into a grudging action, driven by a negotiated mixture or compromise between will and obligation which seems to be the norm in Catalan politics towards support of the governability of Spain. It should be said that, within the terms of the narrative, this obligation affected both parties: 'the PP and the Catalan nationalists are doomed to understand each other so that Aznar can be sworn in as Prime Minister … otherwise it would be suicidal', recommended J.M Sòria from *La Vanguardia* (7 March).

With the benefit of hindsight, this obligation took a step forward just before the final official signature of the pact with the attempt to construct it in terms of logic and fatality: 'The pact … constitutes the most logical, the only viable way out to the political map that emerged after the elections' (*La Vanguardia*, 28 April, by Brunet). The same line was taken by the editorial of the paper itself, which saw the pact not only as a result of the 'logic of parliamentary arithmetic' but of 'logic full stop' (*La Vanguardia*, 28 April). In some cases the pact was presented as 'necessary' (J.M. Brunet, *La Vanguardia*, 14 March), imposed by *force majeure*, as a lesser evil preventing fatal consequences of catastrophic dimensions for the immediate future of the State. Furthermore, according to *La Vanguardia*, this was also the attitude of the grass roots, which although distrustful of the PP, accepted 'the inevitable need for an agreement' (28 March).

Given that the Catalan hero would not be setting off for a struggle with the foe but to make good the lack suffered by the enemy, it is not difficult to understand the importance and even the ideological necessity of the sequence of the granting of 'permission to the hero to leave home', and the heavy qualification of the will to mediate. Turning to external factors such as the results of the elections and its historical consequences; or to re-activate certain values which have become essential part of Catalan identity (such as reason, responsibility, duty etc.), was a strategy to avoid being accused of being opportunistic and having given in (particularly by its own electoral supporters). It was a tactical move to justify help to the former enemy.

Another important part of the strategy was to link the new line of action towards the PP to an attitude coherent with the history of Catalans and Catalanism, thus attempting to prevent the transformation as an opportunistic *ad hoc* adaptation to the new circumstances. And what better attribute than 'pactism'? This concept is another cherished attribute associated not only with Catalanism, but presented as a traditional national trait of the whole of Catalonia. In accordance with this, Oriol Pi de Cabanyes stated in his regular column:

> We Catalans are still attached to the law of pactism, which is, above all ... an ethos. Pactism is a constituent element of the Catalan mentality. To want to pact is to want to get to understand the other, to want to wrap up the deal after negotiating ... but in order to reach an agreement there first has to be some talking and discussing (*La Vanguardia*, 7 March).

Pactism here worked as one of those traditions (whether invented, imagined or reconstructed) meant as a 'set of practices ..., which automatically implies continuity with the past,' (Hobsbawm, 1992: 1). It gave 'the sanction of precedent, social continuity and natural law as expressed in history' (*ibid*: 2), and was used as a 'legitimator of action' (*ibid*: 12).

Moreover, this pactist attitude was made good and justified by one of the self-assigned most important values of Catalan society: Europeanism. As *La Vanguardia* stated in its editorial: 'this scene is very similar to what is normal in other European countries where the need for pacts and the culture of coalition not only do not prevent the formation of governments, but even give a greater feeling of confidence to investors' (10 March).

When these conditions for action were laid out and accepted by the community the hero was allowed to leave home, and *La Vanguardia* subsequently announced: 'Jordi Pujol brought the National Council of his party to an end with a free hand regarding negotiations' (11 March) – that is, the hero's community was presented as having been bestowed its blessing.

The Test

Notwithstanding the permission granted to leave home, the reluctance of the grass roots regarding any negotiation with the PP was borne in mind – 'the swords are still out' (*La Vanguardia*, 11 March). Therefore, the negotiations would not be started on the grounds of a *tabula rasa*. As J. M. Brunet justified: 'what the PP must start getting out of their head is the idea they harboured until a few days ago that they can wipe the slate clean' (*La Vanguardia,* 10 March). The sequence of preparation for the contract involved the establishment, by the Catalanists, of the obligatory conditions (that is, the terms of the contract) that Eternal Spain had to fulfill in order to become a worthy and legitimate partner and power-holder. The whole process constituted a test. And the two characters involved in a test are related in the following manner: 'the hero is tested, interrogated, attacked etc., which prepares the way for his receiving ... a magical agent' (Propp, 1984: 39).

Two points have to be clear at this stage. First of all, the character tested is always the hero. This means that in this narrative, by virtue of the introduction of the test, the former enemy becomes the hero; or the prospective hero, given that the heroic status is recognized only if the test is overcome successfully. Secondly, after the successful completion of the test, the hero obtains 'some agent ... which permits the eventual liquidation' of the lack (*ibid*) – the agent being here CiU's support to form a government.

Significantly the whole process of rapprochement was described by the regular columnist of *La Vanguardia*, González Cabezas as a subtle 'ritual' (*La Vanguardia,* 17 April) in which the PP would have to prove how much it had changed. Furthermore, this test acquired the nature of an unpleasant ordeal. From the outset, the CiU politician Xabier Trias warned the leader of the PP: 'you will find it difficult' (*La Vanguardia,* 8 March); or, as the well-informed editor of the newspaper put it in a mythical sacrifice image: 'Aznar will sweat it out' (*La Vanguardia*, 10 March)[6].

Another implication of the introduction of the test was that the previous asymmetrical relationship between Catalonia and Spain (depicted so far by the narrative), inverted its terms. CiU–Catalonia moved into the position of power, and was now depicted as being able to establish the conditions for the continuation of the political game: for the PP–Eternal Spain, the obligatory aim would be total transformation; for CiU, a reorientation of its discourse would suffice.

The choice of the introduction of the test function itself projected at least two possibilities for the future of the narrative:

• Were the test to be presented as unsuccessful, the villain would remain a villain. Were transformation to be regarded as fake, the villain would become the 'disguised villain' or the 'false hero'.

- Were the transformation to be regarded as successful, the former enemy would have to be accepted as a new hero, a fact that would duplicate the number of heroes with all the implications of the existence of a common space, common values that both would have to share. This scenario stood at odds with the initial confrontation between Catalonia and Eternal Spain, but it was also part and parcel of the grand (and almost mythical) aims of moderate Catalanism encapsulated in the concept '*encaix*' (the fitting in of Catalonia in Spain).

These possible interpretations occurred and will be dealt with in the following pages. The next two sections deal with the contents of the test, the conditions that the PP had to fulfil. They were of a double nature: those set by circumstances and those by the Catalanists themselves.

External Conditions

a) The first two external conditions referred to the actual formation of a government and the nature of such a government. The most important point to account for here is that, in the logic of this narrative, the agent imposing such an obligation and responsibility could not possibly be the Catalanists or Catalonia themselves – it would have been against the logic of the narrative to encourage the villain to gain power. It would be 'the force of circumstance' and 'the will of the people' that would be made to set such obligations. At textual level they were expressed as:

- 'the message of the electorate' (J.M Sòria, *L a Vanguardia*, 7 March)

- 'the reality expressed in the polling booths' (Oriol Pi de Cabanyes, *La Vanguardia*, 7 March)

- 'the results of the recent elections that leave [Mr. Aznar] with no alternative but to put together a pact' (J.M Brunet, *La Vanguardia*, 14 March)

- 'the reality expressed yet again in the elections is that the number of those looking at Spain from a peripheral perspective is growing. In view of this fact ... the most voted-for minority has the main responsibility for constructing a state that will only be feasible if it is shared' (Oriol Pi de Cabanyes, *La Vanguardia* 7 March)

- As in the case of the Catalan nationalists, the narrative depicted the PP as overwhelmed by the obligation of a 'historic opportunity' that the election results implied:

'Spain and Catalonia are at a crossroads of great historic importance. A structural and not merely circumstantial turn is now due. Because the true acknowledgment of the plurality [of the State] demands serious institutional reforms ... and changes of mentality. Because nothing will be consolidated without moving from the culture of confrontation to ... mutual recognition' (Oriol Pi de Cabanyes, *La Vanguardia*, 21 March)

b) The PP was invested with a second *obligation*: acceptance of collaboration with the Catalan nationalists and the implied legitimacy of their role in Spanish politics. These two obligations would, in turn, eliminate their villainous stigma in the rest of Spain. Again (and for the same reasons as before) the source of the obligation was external – the result of the elections: 'the popular and democratic mandate represents a command to reach an agreement with the nationalists' (*La Vanguardia*, 7 March). Oriol Pi de Cabanyes reminded 'the minority majority' (that is, the PP) that they 'had the responsibility to articulate the State, which will only be viable if it is shared' by peripheral nationalists (*La Vanguardia*, 7 March). And *La Vanguardia*, once the pact was almost secured, stated: 'the formerly reviled contribution of the Catalan nationalists to the governability of the State has now become an *obligation* for the PP' (20 March, my italics).

Conditions established by the Catalanists

a) <u>A change in the identity of the PP</u>. According to the political logic of this narrative, the conditions of the pact could not possibly be spelled out in merely political or, even less, in economic terms since his would have triggered the discourse of Catalan blackmail and opportunism.

The conditions involved a transformation of the identity of the PP. Before the elections, Eternal Spain was ruled by a desire to take action, to form a government.

But this will to act was constructed as irrational or untamed, and represented by expressions that depicted the PP as eager 'to gain power at all costs' (J.M. Brunet, *La Vanguardia,* 7 March). The PP was also represented as having strained the situation between the two parties by encouraging interterritorial tension and, more specifically, clear anti-Catalanism. As Brunet put it, '[the PP decided] to bet on an overall majority, to look for it at all costs. And in order to get it they had no qualms about straining the relationship with the nationalist parties' (*ibid*).

As regards the knowledge to hold power, in the first stages of the negotiation, Eternal Spain and its representatives were constructed as keen to take action (to form a government), but with a total lack of understanding of the situation. Let's illustrate this point a little further. In the following text, 'calle Génova' is the Madrid street where the PP headquarters is and where the electoral victory was celebrated. On that street some people were waving pre-Constitutional flags. And from the balcony of the PP headquarters, Mr. Aznar shouted the rather old-fashioned and centralist-sounding 'Long live the King' at the end of his speech:

> How far is Aznar qualified to cope with this pact? The first steps of the potential Prime Minister are really worrying. His harangue from the balcony of calle Génova ... [was] disappointing and gave the impression that they [the PP] had not understood the message of the electorate (J.M. Sòria, *La Vanguardia*, 7 March).

The message being that (according to J. M. Sòria) Spain at that juncture wanted to become a 'plurinational and plurilingual reality' (*ibid*).

In the new situation, CiU and *La Vanguardia* established that if the PP aimed to reach some sort of agreement with the CiU, the former would have to comply with certain conditions. And, furthermore, these conditions were of a cognitive nature: that is, the transformation that Eternal Spain had to undergo, was an obligation set up in terms of cognition, condensed by the political editor of *La Vanguardia* as follows: 'if there is something the PP has to change as from now, it is, above all, its *mentality* ... Aznar must change his *way of thinking* about Catalonia' (*La Vanguardia*, 10 March, my italics). This moment of reflection would be constructed as the potential point in time for a transformation consisting of a renouncing of previous values and the recognition and acceptance of the values of CiU and

Catalonia, that is, a 'change of mentality' (*La Vanguardia* 21 March, by Oriol Pi de Cabanyes).

The possibility of redemption by thoughtful reflection implied that the Eternal Spain of the PP was acting wrongly due to some error of judgement. That is, the deeds of the villainous PP were not carried out 'knowingly and consciously', but in ignorance or 'unknowingly'. This opened the possibility for the discovery of true knowledge and for the regeneration of the PP and Eternal Spain. And that was exactly the purpose of the test: Eternal Spain would have to pass, as an essential obligation, through a series of stages in order to acquire knowledge and an understanding of two 'realities':

a) the multi-national nature of Spain and; b) the historical implications of the new political juncture.

In that test, Eternal Spain would have to re-think its value-system and attitude. Only if reflection resulted in a change of mentality, that is, only after a positive reaction to this cognitive test, would CiU give the 'magical agent' (its 16 votes) to the PP.

The relationship between obligation and knowledge was well exemplified in the following article by Oriol Pi de Cabanyes. For the sake of clarity, I have underlined the linguistic structures of the order of obligation and condition and printed in bold type the expressions belonging to the semantic field of cognition:

> [Aznar] can start where Felipe [González] left off ... – by **acknowledging** that Catalanism is the spirit shared by all Catalan democrats. But he <u>will</u> quickly <u>have to</u> **come to terms with** the fact that in Catalonia, Catalanism, democracy and modernity constitute a conceptual framework radically opposed to what the absolutist Spain has represented throughout history.

> Aznar has a great opportunity. But he <u>must</u> **<u>know</u>** that absolutism is still waiting to be **tamed in the mind**. **<u>And that</u>** in Spain in the idea of a shared State is still weak. **<u>And that</u>** for that reason it is confused with a nation, thought-out in an old-fashioned way – uniform, narrow-minded and expulsionist.

> We are facing a second transition. But nothing will be possible <u>if</u>
> this **perception** does not change, <u>if</u> Spain does not become more
> tolerant regarding its own plurality, <u>if</u> the State is not
> constructed on real instead of fake foundations (*La Vanguardia*,
> 7 March).

Without aiming to analyse this text in detail, some issues should be focused on here. The first one is related to the concept of 'modality' (Fowler, 1991: 85), which includes a range of devices that indicate the attitude to what the speaker actually says. These attitudes fall into the areas of validity, predictability, desirability, obligation, and permission. The modality that predominates in the text is that of 'obligation', expressed by 'have to' and 'must'. This modality places the agents of the Catalanist discourse in an authoritative position with respect to what must be done.

Furthermore, the obligation is based on matters of fact, on reality (hence the reference to the 'real foundations' of the State and the expressive use of the present tense to describe this 'reality'). The inference here is that legitimate power (hence the reference to democracy) requires the prevailing will to exercise power to be modified by means of knowledge; or in other words, knowledge must always precede and determine the will to act. Therefore, the recognition of the transformation of the PP would be made contingent on a process of reflection that would lead to knowledge of reality.

Equally importantly, the obligation entailed a modification of the value-system of the PP. The values which the PP/Eternal Spain had to dispose of were identified by the Catalan nationalists as: absolutism and authoritarianism: 'absolutism is still waiting to be tamed' (Oriol Pi de Cabanyes, 7 March); undemocratic views: 'a worrying deficiency ... of democratic spirit' (*ibid*); intolerance: 'Francoist intolerance', the 'signs of intolerance of recent times' (J. M. Brunet, in *La Vanguardia*, 19 March).

b) <u>Change in the Action of the Subject</u>. The second transformation of the character had to involve a reversal of the action of the PP in its relationship with Catalonia: a modification of its action so as to make it not contradictory with the programme of moderate Catalanism. In this sense, J. M Sòria wrote in his regular column on 7 March that 'a guarantee that insult and defamation will be strongly rejected will have to be demanded' (*La Vanguardia*). And the following day, *La Vanguardia* wrote in the same demanding tone: 'the PP are obliged to leave behind the strategy of confrontation and their defamatory remarks about CiU and to look for more conciliatory formulas ' (8 March); or, as the CiU politician Trias asked Mr. Aznar: 'renew yourself quickly and open up a new culture of dialogue' (*La Vanguardia*, 8 March).

c) Change in the Narrative of the PP: the Alignment with Catalanist Discourse. The transformation in the identity of the PP would have to lead to a change of 'perception' of the moderate Catalanists. In that sense, the political editor of the newspaper, José María Brunet, stated: 'The PP has written too much about "nationalist blackmail"' (*La Vanguardia*, 7 March), adding three days later: 'the conservative leaders will realize as from now that the theory that the nationalists constantly practise the sport of blackmail makes no sense whatsoever' (*La Vanguardia*, 10 March).

Such an alteration would imply a movement towards the alignment of both narratives. If the PP had to bring its narrative of Spain into alignment with that of Catalanism, they would have to admit that Catalonia was not the villain of Spain but its hero – its hero–donor. And indeed, for CiU the most important objective of the negotiation was the 'recognition of the hero' (function 27 of Propp's description), the recognition of CiU and Catalonia as heroes of Spain. This would be tantamount to accepting the Catalanist narrative or Catalanist discourse as real and hegemonic.

It is worth considering in some detail what the public recognition of Catalonia as hero–donor of Spain implied. This self-assigned heroic role is constructed following canonical terms: first of all, 'a difficult task is proposed to the hero' (Propp, 1984: 60); secondly, 'the task is resolved' (Propp, 1984: 60). The idea of moderate Catalanist discourse is that the hero's [Catalonia's] task has already been accomplished in the past and only needs due recognition.

In order to maintain the idea of a Catalonia helping Spain out of her own freedom and autonomy (and not forced by Spain), this 'task' is always constructed as self-imposed. In that sense, one value of Catalonia is made prominent: the self-sacrificial 'sense of state'. Jordi Pujol himself had already stated in the 1960s: 'we have taken part [in the game of the state] ... with poor results compared to the effort we have made' (Pi and Pujol, 1996: 121); an effort that, at times, has been 'futile' and 'laughed at' (*ibid*: 122). One other great historical moment of sacrifice was, according to Pujol, the period of collaboration with the PSOE, a 'tough experience' for which the Spanish political system should be 'thankful' and throughout which CiU had 'so much to put up with' (*La Vanguardia*, 11 March) – in reference to the accusations of blackmail and the supposedly 'anti-Catalan' attitude of the PP during the previous mandate.

The image of an heroic Catalonia almost negating her own interests and wishes for the good of Spain (just the opposite of the 'villain' it was for the PP before the elections) was reproduced in the political juncture after the 1996 elections, which was represented as a new difficult task. The new action of the heroic Catalonia, driven by the idea of sacrifice, was summed up by J. M. Sòria: 'For Pujol the pact is not easy. Someone has said that instead of becoming a key they have been given a cross to bear' (*La Vanguardia*, 7 March) – the key being a reference to CiU's electoral motto. The serious work towards Spain that the concept of 'statesmanship' implies was not only presented as a value non-contradictory to Catalanism but almost exclusive to it. As the regular columnist of *La Vanguardia*, López-Burniol ironically stated, this is an attribute that not even 'the champions of *españolismo*' have: '[t]he sense of State shown by Mr. Pujol – yes, sense of State, which is perfectly compatible with his condition as a Catalan nationalist – is far superior to that of some emphatic champions of the most conventional and noisy *españolismo*' (*La Vanguardia*, 18 February). As will be seen below, José María Aznar, in order to gain CiU's support, took great care in acknowledging Pujol's 'sense of State' and the self-assigned, self-sacrificial nature of Catalonia.

4. The Negative Reaction to the Test

To all these tasks, the potential hero (the PP) reacted (function 13 in Propp's scheme). Of the two types of reaction to the test – 'positive' and 'negative' (Propp, 1984: 123), most the attempts of rapprochement of the PP to CiU between around the 7 and 18 March were regarded as 'negative'. Again, this 'negative' reaction to the test was interpreted in cognitive terms, as an index of a lack of knowledge and understanding. This failure was put down to two main reasons:

a) Lack of political experience. Regarding this point, the political editor of *La Vanguardia* stated that:

> The PP has appeared [at the meetings with CiU] prepared to deal with anything ... But the vagueness of the proposals has surprised those who have spoken to the leaders of the PP ... The PP didn't expect last Sunday's electoral result at all, and that's why it's now sort of groping in the dark. There are still many aspects of power the PP hasn't yet mastered (8 March).

As shown in this short passage, the PP, at the first stages of the negotiation, was still ruled by a will to act ('prepared to deal with anything'), but lacking in the knowledge required to undertake political action, expressed in 'the vagueness of their proposals', 'groping in the dark', or by the reference to the 'many aspects of power the PP hasn't yet mastered'. Along the same lines, *La Vanguardia* headlined one of its reports: 'CiU thinks the PP is muddled but keen to reach a firm agreement' (*La Vanguardia*, 8 March). And it went on to quote one of the Catalanist leaders as saying: the PP 'is extremely keen to reach a firm and stable agreement with CiU but doesn't know the key it has to hit to achieve its objective' (*La Vanguardia*, 8 March). Conversely, CiU and its leaders were represented as having knowledge of the political game through experience (*La Vanguardia*, 6 March, by Joan Barril, opinion editor). The stress here was on the PP's incapacity to deal with power due to a lack of experience. This of course helped towards the construction of an 'incompetent' character – but what I am more interested in here, is lack of knowledge in ideological terms, dealt with next.

b) Lack of knowledge of the reality of Catalonia and of other democratic and European values, which constitute the root of the ideological framework and proposals of the moderate Catalanists. The sudden (but supposedly unthinking) rapprochement of the PP and its supporting media towards the Catalanist postulates was deemed by CiU politician Xabier Trias as 'positive' but 'exaggerated' (*La Vanguardia*, 8 March), that is, beyond truth, reasonableness or any sense of reality and normality.

The discourse became more combative when the financial aspects of the negotiations were attended to. The political editor of *La Vanguardia*, Mr. Brunet, censured the PP for not having comprehended that the pact was not solely to be understood as an economic transaction, and for continuing to perceive the Catalan nationalists as blackmailers. For Brunet, the widespread commonplace of the Catalan blackmail

> has led to the belief that the wallet is enough to obtain the support of Convergència i Unió for the actions of the future government of José María Aznar. And that's not what the whole thing is about. The re-channeling of the situation must start differently, although it is true that the financing of the Autonomies will have to be discussed (*La Vanguardia*, 10 March).

The commonplace (a platitudinous and not thought-through opinion) on which the action of the PP was still supposedly based (combined with the 'exaggerations' of their discourse) reinforced the idea that the PP was not only villainous, but also ignorant. The same idea was expressed by Mr. Barril, for whom the attendant media of the PP showed a total lack of knowledge of the reality of Catalanism by believing that the pact would be guaranteed by fulfilling a certain amount of petty material demands and a few political moves:

> The prophets say that the pact is guaranteed. According to them, it'll be enough for Aznar [to do] a bit of Regional Police deployment, to give them the head of Vidal-Quadras[7] and some reams from Salamanca[8]. In the logic of central government, Pujol is merely a rebellious and tribal obstacle. The Phoenicians[9] also conquered the Mediterranean by exchanging glass beads and trinkets and that's how they established their commercial empire. But that is not what the whole thing is about (7 March).

In order for the test to produce a positive result, the PP had to show awareness that the test was not just an obstacle set up by rebellious tribes, nor simply a barter (hence the reference to the Phoenicians). It was not either a *quid pro quo* of knick-knacks (or small power transference to the regions). It was a real test (with the power asymmetry that a test involves), checking upon knowledge and an ability to exercise power that would only come about after a deep change of identity, action and perception of 'reality' ('what the whole thing is about').

5. The Positive Reaction to the Test: Glorification of the Catalan Hero

On 18 March Pujol and Aznar met in Madrid where the PP leader produced a document with new proposals. According to that document, the PP would commit itself to a further decentralization of the State and the prevalence of the subsidiarity principle. It would involve a transfer of powers to the historical regions and a reform of the fiscal system with a new operation based on financial co-responsibility and inter-territorial solidarity. Furthermore, Mr. Aznar (probably under the pressure of CiU to content its grassroots) went as far as to recognize Catalonia as hero–donor of Spain in the political and in the economic functions. He stated that Catalonia must have a leading role in Spanish politics, given that 'when Catalonia commits herself to the future of Spain, things go well in Spain' (*La Vanguardia*, 19 March). At the same time, the sense of state of Catalan 'non-separatist nationalism' was also recognized by the PP leader as indicative of the importance of Catalan support to the overall Spanish community (*ibid*). The economic counterpart of the Catalan sense of state was recognized by Aznar when he assigned to Catalonia the role of economic powerhouse of the whole of Spain (*La Vanguardia*, 22 March), and admitted that Catalonia had never been lacking in economic solidarity and that it is 'one of the richest communities or countries of Spain that gives most and gets least' (*ibid*)[10]. This suggested the acceptance of another key element of the Catalanist discourse: the 'economic grievance' that Catalonia suffers, and, by implication, the other aspect of Catalonia as a hero – its status as the undeserving victim of a villainous Spain.

The day after such an important meeting between Pujol and Aznar, Lluis Foix (deputy editor of *La Vanguardia*), stated that 'the ceremony of rapprochement has started' (*La Vanguardia*, 19 March). But in general, for *La Vanguardia*, the meeting represented not only a 'rapprochement' but also an alignment of the PP ideology with the narrative programme of moderate Catalanism. According to *La Vanguardia* (22 March), the PP had accepted almost all of the 'nationalist doctrine'. For the sequencing of the narrative, this publicly announced alignment constituted a turning point: the climax of the transformation of Eternal Spain. For *La Vanguardia*, the PP had accepted now the plurinational, plurilingual and pluricultural nature of Spain, and, furthermore (as announced on the front page in *La Vanguardia*, 19 March) it accepted the 'differentiality' of Catalonia in relation to the other regions of Spain. Moreover, it celebrated that the PP would be prepared to accept a 'differentiated development of the Statutes of the Historical Communities' (*ibid*) – all of them long-standing demands of the Catalanists.

In principle, by acknowledging the merits of the most cherished values of moderate Catalanism, the PP now turned the former Catalan villain into a hero – that is, the character that had been previously stigmatized, was now being publicly accepted as a legitimate partner. It was the moment when the Partido Popular was seen as having experienced a kind of 'ideological becoming' (Bakhtin, 1981: 341) after having accepted the 'voice of the other', that is the doctrine of moderate Catalanism. The villainous role of Catalonia, as the character that causes damage to the Spanish community, was dispelled when, as *La Vanguardia* reported, 'Aznar emphatically declared that neither national cohesion nor social cohesion are at risk' in the negotiation with the nationalist minorities (19 March). In the same vein, the political editor of *La Vanguardia* announced that the collaboration of the Catalan nationalists was no longer regarded as involving 'a risk of disintegration of the country' (J. M. Brunet, *La Vanguardia*, 20 March). This transformation was also explicitly highlighted by *La Vanguardia* on its front page: 'the formerly reviled contribution of the Catalan nationalists to the governability of the State' had now turned to a recognition that 'the [electoral] results not only allow, but oblige us to advance towards the guarantee of the presence of Catalan nationalism in the governability of the State' (20 March).

But was the PP's transformation true? This question was the basis for two interpretations of the final development of the events. Some said yes it is true. Some said it was just a farce. These answers led, respectively, to the glorification of the former villain (the PP) and to the revelation of its 'real' identity and its vilification. These two perspectives will be dealt with in the following sections.

6. The PP is the New Spanish Hero: a Success Story

It has been seen that one of the preoccupations of CiU was the transformation of the PP in cognitive terms. As noted before, the first responses to the test were denounced as revealing a lack of understanding of Catalan reality and the multi-national nature of Spain. They were also interpreted as false and 'not enough'. In that sense, *La Vanguardia* wrote: 'cosmetic touches are not enough ... a serious understanding with the most voted for centre party in Catalonia is needed' (*La Vanguardia*, 8 March).

However, after the 19 March meeting between Pujol and Aznar, the political editor of the paper, J. M. Brunet, stated in his political opinion column that the change of attitude 'goes to show that the PP has *known* how to adapt to the circumstances' (*La Vanguardia*, 20 March, my italics). Duran i Lleida also pointed out, in a crucial and well-timed article in *La Vanguardia*: 'the PP is now the first to *recognize* how appropriate it is for the nationalists to make possible the investiture of the government' (20 March, my italics). Just before the formal signing of the pact, *La Vanguardia* acknowledged the new hero on account of having learnt something in what they called 'the psychological battle' (*La Vanguardia*, 28 April). That is, the test that the PP underwent in the narrative was constructed as constituting a cognitive process that resulted in true knowledge.

The narrative construction of events was finally presented as a success in the achievement of the objectives: the recognition of the Catalan subject as hero, and the transformation of the former villain into a legitimate partner in a contract. Aznar, his party, and the Spain they were supposed to represent, despite having been viewed at first as the Francoist and backward villain lacking in knowledge about Catalonia, ended up being praised as a transformed character. This moment represented a type of 'anagnorisis', understood as the point of recognition or discovery. The passage from a state of ignorance to one of knowledge and truth can trigger a new line of action, and that is how the PP was represented: the political editor of *La Vanguardia*, J.M. Brunet, stated that 'the PP [now] accepts Catalan specificity and commits itself to acting accordingly' (*La Vanguardia*, 20 March). The value-system and the actions of the PP were transformed. The test had been a total success.

The possibility of a contract created a common and shared space between the Spanish Right Wing and the Catalan nationalists. In this newly shared universe, the original arrangement of the narrative in terms of 'them' and us' lost its relevance. Consequently, if the space of all the characters was regarded as common, the political fitting of Catalonia ('encaix') was now presented as historically possible. This 'encaix' was made ever more possible by extending the common space to the whole of the Spanish political spectrum: in the well-timed article by Duran i Lleida mentioned above, the Catalanist leader stated that:

> For the first time the Spanish Left and Right agree – even if by force – in the legitimacy of the collaboration of the [Catalan] nationalists; the former because they have already experienced it and the latter because they aspire to reach it … Therefore an

> irreversible step has been taken towards the acceptance of the
> multinationality [of Spain] (*La Vanguardia*, 20 March)

In this success version of the narrative, the Spanish Right had entered the cognitive space of the Catalanists (where admittedly the Left was already situated), leaving behind its negative values and accepting new ones. It is important to note that the negative values had no recipient now, they were not invested in any of the characters, and simply seemed to 'irreversibly' disappear from the narrative universe; or, to put it in Greimas's expressive words, those values disappeared from the semiotic system, they were thrown back 'to their original semantic chaos' (Greimas, 1987: 91).

Following the logic of tales, the character that is subjected to the test is the one that will later be recognized and praised as the hero if the conditions are fulfilled. And here, this narrative seemed to conform to the pattern – the PP was moved on to becoming a hero and publicly glorified. In that sense, only days after the formation of the new central government, Pujol summed up and approved publicly the veracity of the transformation:

> the Spanish Right had to consider its conception of Spain which
> until now had been related to ... the Catholic Monarchs. The PP
> now accepts the plurinational reality. And it is to Aznar's credit
> that the Spanish Right now respects Catalonia and the Basque
> Country (*La Vanguardia,* 7 May).

La Vanguardia equally highlighted this public recognition in the headline–quotation 'What Aznar has done is very commendable' (7 May). Therefore, after the PP's recognition of the heroic status of Catalonia, CiU itself acknowledged the heroic status of the PP in a move towards the 'mutual recognition' that had been urged before (Oriol de Cabanyes, *La Vanguardia*, 21 March), and which stands on its own as a requirement for the achievement of any type of contract.

What commenced as a fierce confrontation, ended with reconciliation. The tragic overtones of the beginning had been transformed into a settlement whereby the 'bitterest enemies in the piece ... walk off good friends at the end, with no slaying of anyone by anyone', a move that belongs to the realm of comedy (Aristotle, 1924:

1453). And this was a comic touch that did not go unnoticed by the critics of the final pact.

7. The PP is the Disguised Villain: a Story of Trickery

If the PP, constructed at the beginning as unable to 'comprehend', had been turned into a hero after its process of reflection, those critical to the pact (within *La Vanguardia* itself), insisted in the roguish nature of the PP. If the story of success progressed towards and finally ended up with a 'glorification' of the new hero, this one opted *all along* for its 'disqualification', a process that would be carried out on the grounds of the mendacity of the subject (only pretending to have 'changed'). In that sense, Mr. Sòria ironically stated in an article significantly entitled 'Whatever suits best': 'the former blackmail is now nothing other than an exercise in responsibility. The former Spain of the auction-house is now a culture of coalition' (14 March). That is: the PP and its co-attendant media no longer presented blackmailing and auctioning as the values that rule the action of Catalonia. But there was a clear misgiving about this transformation:

> But until when? Is so much reasonableness credible? And what
> if Pujol says no? And what if CiU refuses to listen and Aznar
> needed the PSOE's abstention to be sworn in? They'll go back to
> war (*La Vanguardia*, 14 March).

This interpretation of the action suggested that the transformation the PP was supposedly undergoing was insincere, carried out through necessity, and out of a desperate will to grab power. It was, in the words of Miquel Serrallès, the editor of the nationalist magazine *Debat Nacionalista,* 'a conversion to Catalanism driven by self-interest ... a conversion of persons and institutions driven by simple opportunism' (*La Vanguardia,* 14 March). Or, in the words of the columnist Baltasar Porcel:

> such smiles could be just an exercise in cynicism in order to get
> hold of power at all costs – with the voters, MPs and the furious
> writers and supporting *tertulieros*[11] knowing that at the earliest
> opportunity they will go back to the their old primitive ways[12]
> (*La Vanguardia*, 11 March).

It must be added that the accusations of mendacity were not particular to this period of Spanish history. Pujol remarked in 1978 that the Catalans:

> have not been happy not for not having attained our objectives, nor for having lost, but for something even worse ... The game we have been offered has always been a cheating game, a game where a great effort was repaid with a tiny reward, or no reward at all (Pi and Pujol, 1996: 120–121).

'Cynicism', 'opportunism', 'self-interest' or 'simulation' (González Cabezas, *La Vanguardia,* 27 March) and 'pantomime of cordiality' (Baltasar Porcel, *La Vanguardia,* 25 March) were only some of the ways of constructing the character as a 'villain in disguise' and of exposing its intentions and real identity. Referring back to the model put forward by Propp, this would constitute the function defined as 'trickery'. In this sequence the villain, acting in disguise, 'attempts to deceive his victim' (Propp, 1984: 29). In this case, the objective of the PP–Eternal Spain would have been to persuade Catalonia of the acceptance of a *true* transformation that was in fact a *lie*. Because of this deception, for the critics of the pact the PP remained ineligible or illegitimate for the pact. This interpretation acted as a block for the development of the narrative transformation and, in some way, returned the narrative back to its initial position of confrontation with the enemy.

This interpretation of the PP's actions was not limited to accomplished facts. If we return to Mr. Sòria's and Mr. Porcel's syntactically identical utterances, 'they'll go back to war' and 'they'll go back to their primitive old ways', we discover a prospective and almost prophetic-sounding knowledge about the actions of Eternal Spain. It is a knowledge based on what has been seen before, of what is already known, and of what can be expected of the Spain that never changes[13].

For those voices cynical of the whole process of negotiation, the final wedding function (the last one in a fairy tale and the one that symbolizes success) was qualified as a 'spectacular marriage of convenience' (González Cabezas, *La Vanguardia,* 17 April). This 'marriage of convenience' was celebrated not out of conviction on the part of the PP (that is, not out of having understood or realized the 'truth' or 'validity' of Catalan demands and the whole process of change), but, rather, out of necessity in their eagerness to gain political power. CiU did not escape this criticism:

> Obviously, the marriage is born out of necessity rather than love, but it is known that interest can be a stronger and longer lasting bond than love and desire. It's not by chance that these times are more keen on the prose of accounting than on romantic poetry ... Since there is no love, only money will count (Gónzalez Cabezas, *La Vanguardia*, 17 April).

8. Strategic Anti-Catalanism: the Irredeemable Spain

In the previous section, it was discussed how the 'success story' was counterbalanced by a narrative variation governed by the idea of a cunning PP. This negation of the success variation was further stressed after the PSOE made its first criticism of the prospective pact, when the test was represented as yielding its first 'positive response'. For Socialist politicians, the process was not a turning point of historical proportions brought about by the transformation of the Right. It was simply an economic negotiation and 'the result of the weakness' of the PP (*La Vanguardia*, quoting Ramón Jáuregui, leader of the Basque Socialists–PSOE, 18 March). The Right was accused of 'appeasement' (*ibid*); and the negotiation between the PP and CiU was deemed as being led by a 'mercantilist attitude' (*ibid*), since:

> all the claims being taken care of represent a bigger flow of money towards the Basque Country and Catalonia and the future of Spain is never discussed in relation to questions as important as unemployment or the fulfillment of the Maastricht criteria (*ibid*).

The PP interpreted such disapproval in strict political terms as 'an attempt by the PSOE to prevent the negotiations from coming to something' (*La Vanguardia*, 19 March). However, for Catalanists the Socialist attitude had a national and historical resonance. This attitude, they argued, was the result of a long-standing anti-Catalan stance, still prevalent in the rest of Spain, which dictates that Catalonia must not intervene in the affairs of the State. In this critical line, the sense of closure and end of conflict, together with the idea that certain ideas had disappeared for ever from the Spanish universe (seen in the success story), were offset by an interpretation of the events stemming from the following premise: values do not disappear but simply become 'dormant' – to use Barthes's words (1972: 144) – or 'virtual', to use Greimas's (1987: 101).

This interpretation picked up the original pattern of the narrative but with a change in the actors that fulfilled the roles: the PSOE, praised at the beginning for its understanding of the nationalist cause (and fulfilling the role of the donor) was now moved to the role of villain. On 19 March, the columnist Baltasar Porcel commented on the changes of attitude of the Socialists: 'the PSOE has become alarmed and has decided to go back to its old anti-Catalanist activity in a swift substitution of the PP in such a task' as herald of the 'Unity of Spain', and as condemner of the fact that 'a Catalan party wants to have a say in Spain. Which, of course, is not vetoed by the Constitution' (*La Vanguardia*).

This extract indicates a redefinition from the role of donor back into the interchangeable role of villain; and also goes to show the supposedly 'dormant' status of the anti-Catalanist values ('its old activity'). In this interpretation, the PSOE was thus accused of dusting down its old anti-Catalanism, and of its 'anti-Catalan re-release' (Carlos Sentís, *La Vanguardia*, 20 March). The Socialists became stigmatized with the same value of anti-Catalanism as the PP was at the beginning.

And furthermore, Baltasar Porcel, wondering about the sudden changes of attitude of PP and PSOE towards the Catalanists, wrote:

> Why are PSOE and PP so obstinately trying to deceive the citizens of this old Fatherland of Don Pelayo and the Civil Wars?[14] It's a mystery. [So far they have tried and managed] to get Spaniards to believe that yesterday's devil is today's angel, and vice versa (*La Vanguardia*, 19 March).

In this extract it is clear that the author is rejecting the tripartite actantial organization on which the 'story of success' of *La Vanguardia* was based (hero, villain, and donor). He is substituting it by a bipolar one: there is just a hero and a villain. The message here is that the positions of donor and villain are simply circumstantial and interchangeable roles depending on the political context. In Propp's own words it would be a case of 'distribution of a single sphere of action among several characters' (1984: 81). In other words, a case of just one role (the villain) being segmented into two actors (PSOE and the PP) having the same narrative programme but becoming helpers of CiU/Catalonia when the circumstances call for it. This double-role character fits into the category of the *pícaro* (the *picaresque* being, incidentally, a very Spanish genre) who, as Bakhtin points out, 'is not implicated in any norm, requirement, ideal; he is not of one piece and is not consistent ... [he] is faithful to nothing, he betrays everything – but he is nevertheless true to himself, to his own orientation' (Bakhtin, 1981: 408).

This interpretation of events was, thus, carried out along the lines of a 'virtuality'. Paraphrasing Greimas, it can be said that the transformation is only 'virtual' if, after having acquired a new value, the character still remains 'attracted' to the value it has just renounced, maintaining the possibility of a renewed conjunction with it (1987: 103). This is the idea expressed by one of the editors of *La Vanguardia*, Carlos Sentís, in his comment about the transference of the negative value of anti-Catalanism (and, one might add, all the values related to it) between the two major Spanish parties:

> anti-Catalanism in Spain ... is used from opposition and, then, once in power it is put in the cupboard. The choir of Socialist barons helps us to forget the PP's anti-Catalanism, also opportunistic, and, therefore, removable (*La Vanguardia*, 20 March).

The narrative variation of success constituted the end of the Two Spains. There was now one Spain that was European, democratic and modern, a Spain where Catalonia could fit in. In the critical interpretation of the events, the PP (the Right) and the PSOE (the Left) were depicted as two characters performing the same role. This constituted, again, the end of the discourse of the Two Spains, but the reverse of the one depicted in the successful interpretation of the events – the Two Spains being in fact just one irregenerable Spain whose ideological universe is opposite to the Catalan.

It is interesting to note that the first pact between CiU and PSOE underwent the same type of analysis by, for example, the Catalan (and Catalanist one should add) sociologist Cardús for whom the Socialists were, before the 1982 general election (their first victory), the heralds of the 'recovery of Spanish pride' (Cardús, 1995: 25). Throughout their successive governments, Cardús argued, the Socialists 'showed very little will to recognize the national diversity of the State' (*ibid*: 25), and only after having lost their overall majority in 1993, and seeing themselves in need of CiU's parliamentary support, did they start to show any respect for the peripheral nationalists. And the author (with prophetic-sounding rhetoric) added: 'the conversion is so much driven by self-interest that I don't think it is far-fetched to say that they may eventually lose their friendliness and good manners towards the Basque and Catalan nationalists' (*ibid*).

9. Spain: The Perseverance of Ignorance

Even where the attitude of the PSOE was not condemned as trickery, the idea of the persistence of an irregenerable and irredeemable Spain was continued by the interpretation of the Socialist attitude as ignorant. The Catalan nationalist politician López de Lerma interpreted the PSOE's arguable move to anti-Catalanism as within 'the traditional perspective of *lack of understanding* of the participation of Catalanism in Spanish politics' (*La Vanguardia,* 20 March, my italics). The deputy editor of *La Vanguardia*, Lluis Foix, carried out a similar interpretation of the events. He wrote about the supposed long-standing lack of understanding of the political reality of Spain, as an attribute of the whole of Spanish society:

> what the Socialists are asking about now is the costs ... And those who thought that the Right was the only one against dialogue and negotiation with the peripheral nationalisms will realize that we'll get a similar rhetoric from well-qualified sectors of Socialism. The problem does not lie in parties but in the nature of a society with a historical lack of understanding towards the peripheral differences' (*La Vanguardia*, 18 March).

Yet again the supposed incompatibility between the ideological universes of Catalonia and Spain was made evident, such irreconcilability being constructed as the product of a long-standing and unsolvable lack of knowledge.

10. The Roles of Catalonia

It is interesting to note that the success-story variation of the narrative covered the role of the Catalan hero in two ways, consistent with what was established by Propp in his seminal study: as the sufferer of the actions of the villain (or victim hero), first, and, later on, as the one who agrees to liquidate the misfortune or lack of another character (Propp, 1984: 50). Furthermore, the Catalan hero fulfilled the role of the donor by setting a test to the PP in order to prepare it for the transmission of the agent (the 16 votes of CiU).

In that test, one element was hammered home: it was thanks to the transforming power of CiU and Catalonia that the conversion of the former enemy into a legitimate partner was made possible. This key role granted to Catalonia in the Spain–Catalonia relationship can be further explained by looking into the insights of Frederic Jameson in *The Prison-House of Language* (1974). Jameson offers a new perspective of Propp's formal scheme and ventures that 'the centre of gravity of the narrated events lies not in the fact of the change, but in the explanation of the change, in the middle term which modulates from one state to the other' (Jameson, 1974: 67). This new perspective places the highest importance on the figure of the donor, who becomes, then:

> the element which explains the changes described in the story ... and which is therefore somehow responsible for the 'storiness' of the story in the first place. Thus, the satisfaction and the completeness of the tale comes not from the fact that the hero manages to rescue the princess in the end, but rather the means or agent given him to do so: what Propp's discovery implies is that every How (the magical agent) always conceals a Who (the donor), that somewhere hidden in the very structure of the story itself stands the human figure of a mediator (*ibid*).

The same author spells out the importance of the existence of such a mediator in the following terms:

> in the beginning the hero is never strong enough to conquer by himself. He suffers from some initial lack of being: either he is simply not strong enough or not courageous enough, or else he is too naive and simple-minded to know what to do with his strength. The donor is the complement, the reverse, of this basic ontological weakness (*ibid*: 67–68).

It has been seen how the initial relationship between Catalonia and the rest of Spain was represented at as 'a head-on direct one of ... hatred or conflict' (*ibid*: 1974: 68). However, the focus later moved to the 'lateral relationship of the hero [in this case the prospective hero, PP–Eternal Spain] to the ex-centric figure of the donor [Catalonia]' (*ibid*: 1974: 68), which 'helped' Spain transform and surmount its 'ontological weakness'. Catalonia assisted the PP and the whole of Spain through their rite of passage and onto the democratic, modern and civilized world.

This double role of Catalonia as hero–victim and hero–donor is not a contradiction, but the result of being present in two 'spheres of action' (Propp, 1984: 48). It is significant that both kinds of heroes are not to be found performed by the same character in any of the tales analysed by Propp (Asa Berger, 1997: 27). However, the double nature of a character acting as victim and redeemer is not unheard of. It is, indeed, one the main features of messianic stories. In the moderate Catalanist discourse, Catalonia adopts the redeeming role of the 'chosen', whose sufferings are destined to change the ontological status of Spain (that is villainous out of a lack of knowledge). The self-sacrifice of Catalonia (driven by pactism, responsibility and sense of state) has an elevated objective: the mythical *encaix*, the harmonious political and administrative fitting in of Catalonia within Spain. This dream of peaceful 'living-together' echoes the myth of the Golden Age, the end of conflict.

Let's consider now the unsuccessful variation of the narrative, the one governed by the idea of Spanish opportunism and trickery. In this case two possibilities should be investigated: a) whether Catalonia was fulfilling the role of the victim 'that submits to deception and thereby unwittingly helps the enemy' (the 'complicity' function) (Propp, 1984: 30); or b) whether CiU/Catalonia were keen to accept a pact with the PP despite the fact of being aware of the mendacity of the PP. Let's take the following text as a comment on such a relationship:

> The PP or Aznar, what are they up to? Cleopatra, in order to seduce Julius Caesar, offered herself clad in silky oriental garments; in order to gulp down Anthony she appeared rocking herself on a golden bench; and in order to captivate Augustus she lay down on a humble straw mattress dressed in just a tunic. Of course, the latter, who was, moreover, cold and severe, was the only one to resist her. Aznar must have learnt this lesson or a similar one and is now Catalanizing lavishly. But is he actually

seducing anyone? It doesn't seem so. The conversion smells too fishy. But since politics is in the end just a series of one-off verbal statements in a changing scene, an unexpected pantomime of cordiality has been created which is smoothing down the rough edges of the spectators. The atmosphere in Catalonia is ironic, skeptical and bland; and it is already a general belief that there had to be a pact. Cleopatra ... won.

Until Augustus. And then she had to commit suicide (Baltasar Porcel, *La Vanguardia,* 25 March).

This text is very critical of the pact. In Mr. Porcel's metaphor, the role of Cleopatra is identified with the PP and its leader, Mr. Aznar. And CiU and its leader, Jordi Pujol, play the metaphorical roles of Julius Caesar or Anthony, since they all ended up seduced. But in this text the relationship established between the PP and CiU does not seem to be one driven by love or seduction, but based on mendacity on the part of the two characters. On the one hand, the PP tries to seduce with a false ('fishy') conversion. On the other, Pujol, by being part of the 'pantomime of cordiality', is also driven in his actions by mendacity. Pujol receives another criticism that was so far reserved for the Spanish Right (or even Spanish political parties in general): opportunism ('politics is in the end just a series of one-off verbal statements'). In its desire to legitimise the pact, CiU, according to the author, managed to convince Catalan public opinion of the inevitability of the pact: 'and it is already a general belief that there had to be a pact'. The final sentence is, therefore, victory for the Spanish Right and a yet another defeat for Catalonia: 'Cleopatra won'.

However, despite the act of persuasion by CiU on Catalan public opinion, the 'cold and severe' Catalonia (Augustus), understood as the people (or 'the atmosphere in Catalonia'), are not really deceived. Real Catalonia (the people of Catalonia) stays aside and watches. Its mood is constructed in three different ways by the sentence – 'the atmosphere in Catalonia is ironic, skeptical and bland', which denotes:

a) Sarcastic distance. The adjective 'ironic' expresses an attitude of mockery on facing the incongruity of a situation where two previously opposed worlds meet.

b) Incredulity. The adjective 'skeptical' expresses the disbelief of Catalonia towards the transformation of the old enemy into the new hero.

c) Aphoria. 'Bland' expresses what Greimas calls 'aphoria', meaning neither euphoria nor dysphoria (Greimas, 1976: 158).

Faced with the pact, real Catalonia remained still, tranquil, even-tempered – all images that reproduced the strongly established myth of the 'Catalan oasis' and reinforced the idea of the perseverance of the being of Catalonia and the lack of perturbances despite the events being narrated.

11. Epilogue: After the 2000 Elections

Pre-electoral Campaign

Just as in 1996, in the campaign before the 12 March 2000 election there was a turning point in the attitude of CiU towards PP marked by the publication of surveys between 3 and 5 March. Before these surveys, none of the main all-Spanish parties were forecast to get close to overall majority. In that juncture, CiU adopted a clear softly-softly approach towards the PP. That attitude was reciprocated by the PP, which could not afford to lose the support of Catalanists. *La Vanguardia* was at times clearly backing a victory of the PP in the whole of Spain for the following reasons: a) the more radicalized the campaign was, the more difficult it would have been to call for the tactical vote in favour of CiU; b) a radical campaign against the PP would have jeopardized the support of the PP to CiU in the Catalan parliament, where the Catalanists had a minority government; and c) experience had shown that collaborating with another centre–right party, such as the PP, is more fruitful for the interests of centre–right Catalanism than working with the PSOE.

The surveys predicted a victory for the PP, 8 to 12 MPs short of an overall majority. The same surveys also gave 14 to 15 parliamentary seats for CiU. But the fear of a possible overall majority triggered a renewed attack by CiU against the PP. A complete demonization of a Francoist PP would have been beyond belief for analysts and grassroots after four years of collaboration. However, as in 1996, the traditional misgivings of Catalanists about the sensitivity of Spanish society regarding the plurality of Spain were present again. The CiU politician, Xabier Trias, stated:

'I think that Almunia' (the socialist candidate to PM)
is proving to be more insensitive [to the idea of a plurinational
Spain], but I have my doubts about what would happen if
Aznar were not in office. This is a phenomenon of
transmutation where the Socialists and the PP, according to
whether they are in the Government or in the opposition,
behave this way or the other. But deep inside they are the same
(*La Vanguardia*, 8 March 2000).

For a Catalanist party this should leave the door closed for future collaboration with both the Right and the Left. Or the opposite: since they are both the same, CiU could leave the door open to future collaborations with either of the main parties. This was, of course, at the risk of being accused of opportunism. But the accusations of hypocrisy and opportunism, as we have seen above, can be compensated with the grand idea of the moderating role of Catalonia in Spanish politics. And, as in 1996, that was precisely what happened in 2000: in the case of an insufficient victory of the PP (the argument went), CiU would be essential to prevent Aznar's party from 'carrying out its right-wing programme' (*La Vanguardia*, 6 March 2000), since as Duran i Lleida put it 'we are the only ones who can curb the excesses of the PP' (*La Vanguardia*, 3 March 2000).

These attacks, however, were not the norm in the attitude of CiU and *La Vanguardia* towards the PP. Indeed, there were few opinion articles on the elections (nothing compared to 1996) and very few with an anti-PP tone. Quite the opposite, in fact. The editorial of 6 March praised the economic and political sucesses of the PP Government. On 12 March 2000, the editor of *La Vanguardia*, Juan Tàpia, praised the PP Government for achieving economic growth, for the succesful entry of Spain into the euro zone and for the political stability (all of this thanks to the pact with CiU, of course). It was quite clear where *La Vanguardia*'s sympathies were. The possibility of a new PP–CiU tandem was even praised by Baltasar Porcel, so anti-PP in 1996: 'The best verdict of the ballot box' he claimed 'would be the victory of the PP because they've done it alright'. However, Porcel warned of the 'catastrophic' consequences of an overall majority for the plurality of Spain; '[h]ence' Porcel concluded 'the ideal scenario would be a PP in need of CiU' (5 March, 2000). As in 1996, the idea of a Catalonia redeeming Spain from catastrophe was being reproduced.

The PP's Overall Majority

In the elections the share of Parliamentary seats was as follows:

Political Party	Seats
PP	183
PSOE	125
CiU	15
IU	8
PNV	7
Coalición Canaria	4
BNG	3

In Catalonia the results were:

Political Party	Seats
PSOE	17
CiU	15
PP	12
ERC	1
IC–IU	1

These results meant that, for the first time after Franco's death, a right-wing party managed to get an overall majority.

There were clear differences with 1996, the most important being that CiU or other peripheral nationalists were not needed by the PP to form a Government. However, Aznar publicly announced his intention, despite his overall majority, of reaching an agreement with the Canarian Nationalists and CiU (even offering a ministry to the Catalanists). This was a clever move with the three-fold intention of a) giving an image of moderation; b) preventing the radicalization of peripheral nationalists; and c) gathering the support of the whole of the Right in Spain (Canarian nationalists are also regarded as centre–right). Incidentally, the Basque Nationalists of PNV were excluded from the offer on account of their radical attitude towards independence of the Basque Country. And not only did the PP establish a distance with the PNV. CiU also, together with *La Vanguardia*, reinforced their distance from the more radical Basque Nationalists and the Basque Country in general: 'Our political tradition, our situation, is not the same as the Basque ones', said the columnist Pi de Cabanyes (*La Vanguardia*, 23 March 2000), in justification of the moderate stance towards the PP and its offer of a pact. Xabier Bru de Sala (close to the PSOE) also entered the fray with an article dramatically entitled 'Antithetical peoples' in which he stated that:

> the forms of life particular to Catalonia are opposed to the Basque ones ... Let's compare ourselves as Catalans to the Andalusians, the Portuguese or the Italians and we will find many similarities. They all disappear when we compare ourselves to the Basques ... We might have faults, but us Catalans are more open to negotiation ... We have been looking for common spaces for at least a century, which is the opposite of division and confrontation (*La Vanguardia*, 4 June 2000).

The Glorification of the Catalanized PP

After the 1996 elections the Catalan nationalists were in a position of power and could develop the discourse of a test, an ordeal whereby the PP had to prove that it had changed and had accepted an alignment with the Catalanist discourse. But now there was no possibility of recourse to a test, since CiU was not needed anyway. Without the test, the narrative picked up where it was left off in 1996, in the sequence of glorification. The 13 March 2000 editorial of *La Vanguardia* explained the triumph of the PP on account of its economic, social and political successes, and Baltasar Porcel praised its 'outstanding performance in office' in his daily column on 14 March.

The yard-stick for this glorification was the degree of 'catalanization' of the PP and of Spain as a whole. The idea of the catalanization of Spain was cleverly picked up by José María Aznar. In a well-timed interview published by *La Vanguardia* just before the elections, he stated that: 'The balance-sheet of our collaboration with the nationalists is positive and my desire is for its continuation in the future'; and going on about the four–year term he added:

what we have achieved in these years is an open, competitive and moderate Spain, such as many Catalans have always wanted ... The Catalan mentality is triumphing in Spain and Catalans triumph in Spain. And I insist: the Catalan concept of Spain, the idea of an open, European, modern and competitive country is triumphing in Spain as well (5 March 2000).

The columnists of *La Vanguardia* readily sang along to this tune and reciprocated by judging the PP on attributes traditionally reserved for Catalonia and Catalan politics. On 16 March, Oriol Pi de Cabanyes praised the 'sensibleness and constructive spirit' of the PP – two characteristics reserved for Catalans until then. The political editor of *La Vanguardia*, J.M. Brunet, stated that

the PP has shown great flexibility to maintain a dialogue and reach agreements. Aznar proved it in 1996, when there was no experience of relationships with the nationalists ... Aznar talks in terms of Spanish plurality, the PP has come to terms with that reality and all its consequences. This is a step of a historical dimension (*La Vanguardia*, 19 March 2000).

J. M. Brunet even put down Aznar's victory to his 'defence of the plural Spain' in his column; and he went on: 'the citizens have rewarded that democratic strength', despite the fact that the undemocratic spirit of the PP was precisely the reason for the reluctance to envisage a pact in 1996. For Baltasar Porcel all the fears about the PP swinging its 'scythe' (with its connotations of death) had been proved unfounded (20 March 2000).

The Historical Dimension of the Elections: Shedding the Past

Because of the dualistic attitude of CiU towards Spain, pacts with all-Spanish parties almost invariably have to be explained away in terms of historical events affecting the structure of the state and the identity of Spain. Even at the risk of diverting from the line of analysis, I would like to note that this stance is not new in the history of Catalanism. Without intending to establish direct links between CiU and other parties from the past (because of different ideological and historical circumstances), a continuity with the line of action taken by La Lliga Regionalista of Prat de la Riba and Cambó can be identified[15]. The political manifesto 'For Catalonia and a Greater Spain' (written and published in 1916 by Prat de la Riba and Cambó and signed by other Catalanist politicians) set out to justify the intervention of Catalanists in the affairs of the central Government against the background of a specific historical moment: the First World War. Just as in the analyses provided above, Catalonia was then presented as 'victim' of Spain, but it was from Catalonia that the redemption of Spain was offered (in a tone that was tender and loving, but also messianic and at times apocalyptic).

The manifesto urged restructuring towards a greater Spain, based on what were presented as solid facts: the war being fought out then 'was the triumph of the unifying and cohesive value of nationalism and autonomy' (Ainaud de Lasarte, 1966: 174), as in the cases of Germany and Austria–Hungary, and the British Empire. In contrast the manifesto highlighted that 'the absolute inefficency, the total sterility of the Spanish Government' (*ibid*: 166) in the past, in the present and in its prospects for the future was due to the 'central problem of Spanish life': its constitution (*ibid*). Spain, according to the manifesto was 'lacking in structure and coordination, and hence in spiritual cohesion' (*ibid*). The solution to the problem was that all regions be treated on an equal footing (*ibid*: 167) in order to promote 'the greatness of Spain' (*ibid*: 169). The manifesto insisted that if Spain wished to participate and intervene in the new international order, she would have to integrate harmoniously all the nations comprised in it. Spain had to 'understand the exceptional nature of the moment … the heroic moment we are passing through' (*ibid*: 177)

The context of an international war and a new world order cannot be compared to the domestic political circumstances of the periods analysed here, but the recourse to the strategy of the 'exceptionality of the moment' is very similar. It has been seen how in 1993 CiU justified its pact with PSOE in order to provide the necessary political stability needed for preparing for Spain's entry into the European monetary union (which was of utmost importance for Spanish politicians, almost a test of national pride). In 1996 the pact was explained away under the banner of the restructuring of Spain in preparation for the XXI century (with further integration within the EU on the background).

In a clear process of synergy between the Spanish Centre–right and moderate Catalanism, in 2000 there was agreement between *La Vanguardia* and the PP in the interpretation of the historical dimension of the elections. On the night of the overall victory José María Aznar privately told the director of *El Mundo*, Pedro J. Ramírez, that the results meant 'the end of the Civil War' (Sahagún, 2001: 379). The leader of the PP also stated that 'Spain has turned the page' and now 'neither the old quarrels nor the old sectarianisms ... nor the absence of a project for Spain will dominate the future of Spain' (*La Vanguardia*, 16 March 2000).

Interestingly enough, the columnist Consuelo Sánchez-Vicente made the following statement along the same lines: 'the historical victory of the PP ... could well mean the sociological end of our terrible Civil War and our no less horrible post-war period' (*La Vanguardia*, 14 March 2000). These statements are in the same line as what was seen in the epilogue to chapter 2: the haunting nature of the Francoist past in Spanish politics and the desire to shed it. It is true to say that Sánchez-Vicente's opinion could not be regarded as representative of *La Vanguardia*; firstly, because it was the only article to express such an idea, and, secondly because she is from Madrid and could not possibly qualify as a mouthpiece of Catalanism.

However, the interpretation of the new circumstances as a 'new era' (where traces of Francoism have disappeared and the previous qualms about agreeing with a party regarded as the heirs of Franco were now dispelled), was pivotal in the justification of the new pact. If in 1996 Catalanist discourse only had to 'reorientate' itself to adapt to the new circumstances, in 2000 the so-called radical transformation in Spanish society affected Catalonia to a similar degree. That was the message from CiU and that was the message from *La Vanguardia*: if Spain had left its past behind so must Catalonia – and resistance must give way to agreement. On 14 March 2000, the key CiU politician, Roca i Junyent, in an article entitled 'Above all, dialogue' justified an acceptance of Aznar's offer of a political agreement by stating that the PP's overall majority meant 'an important change in Spanish political life, not only towards the future but also as a moment of reflection about the past': in other words, the PP could not be regarded as the heir of Francoism anymore. And for Catalonia, he had this message:

entrenching ourselves in Catalonia would be a mistake, to turn Catalonia into a bulwark of the reconquest of we-don't-know-what-exactly would be to renounce exemplary behaviour of a society which is aware of its difference (as shown in the elections) but which does not want to be out of the general progress of Spain, to which it has contributed with its decisive participation.

Again, agreement with the rest of Spain was the name of the game. And in its justification, 'the past' was a pivotal element: the idea of resistance was rejected not only because it is part of the past (hence the mention of the reconquest) but also due to the vagueness of its contents – 'we-don't-know-what-exactly'. This small pasage constitutes a clear defence of two main interrelated elements of Catalanism regarding the relationship between Spain and Catalonia: albeit different from the rest of country, Catalonia has aspirations within Spain, where it has performed a decisive and exemplary role.

In preparation for the delegitimation of those opposed to the pact, Oriol Pi de Cabanyes also made use of the past/present dichotomy. He distinguished the new and the old nationalism – and he advocated:

> abandoning the 'comfortable and traditional' resistence typical of the 'lefties', followers of the spirit of antifrancoism, which would place Catalonia in permanent oposition to Central Government. The new attitude for Catalanism is agreement with Madrid. Now it's not about transforming ... but developing what already exists towards higher levels of shared welfare' (*La Vanguardia*, 23 March 2000).

Again, the pre-democratic past and the political practices of that period were used to delegitimize those more radical sections of Catalanism. And if in 1996 there was still a lot to change and even redeem in Spanish society, now it was just a matter of improving the shared space.

A New Pact with the Irredeemable Spain

There was at least one voice expressing disapproval. For Manuel Trallero (who was also clearly anti-PP in 1996), the Spain of 2000 was not a common space for all to share, but just the state which 'at the end of the day has canons and the machinery to mint money' (*La Vanguardia*, 20 March 2000). For Trallero, in the 2000 election, 'they got rid of us Catalans ... and we have been left all dressed up and nowhere to go' (*La Vanguardia*, 14 March 2000). Since Aznar offered dialogue to the Catalanists from the first day, the 'they' Trallero is referring to is not the PP but Spanish voters, Spanish society: indeed, he was just reproducing the idea of an anti-Catalanism supposedly entrenched in the whole of Spanish society. For him, getting rid of the 'Catalans' produced a 'joy' which 'has no political colour, it is very widespread, it is deeply rooted in wide sectors of the population' (*ibid*).

As in 1996, the event that triggered such an idea was the comment of some politicians of the PSOE and some left-wing union leaders, who put down the defeat of the Left to the lack of a vision of Spain and the absence of a project for the whole of the country. Whereas in the rest of the daily no one reacted to these comments, Manuel Trallero wrote, with fearmongering rhetoric, remembering the Civil War: 'The Nationals are back' (the Nationals being the Francoist side in the war). For Trallero, the Civil War was clearly far from over. On the contrary, for him mentioning the lack of a Spanish project meant 'a return to the Imperial idea of the Fatherland, a Spain imposed by legal fiat' (*La Vanguardia*, 17 April 2000). Grouping the socialists with the Francoist troops is an absurd idea that only goes to show the power of the ghost of Franco, which is used in Spain as a delegitimizing tool for anything and everything.

In 1996, a strong anti-pact narrative stream found expression in *La Vanguardia*. This time round, Trallero was virtually the only (albeit vociferous) columnist to express his contrary stance to the CiU–PP agreement. Despite normally displaying a clear editorial stance, all newspapers are aware that there is a less conformist section of their readership that needs to be catered for. And Trallero played that role here. In his columns, not only the PP and the Spanish socialists were attacked. Trallero's sarcastic comments were also aimed at CiU and the ease with which their idea of Spain and the role of Catalonia in the whole of the country changes according to the circumstances. On 16 April he wrote:

we are part of a thing called Spain which until not long ago I heard them say did not exist ... that it was just visions, that they had made it up ... This is the sublime moment of great spiritual intensity, in which any observer paying close attention to reality might have the feeling that politics bears a weird resemblance to a circus (*La Vanguardia*, 16 April 2000).

If for CiU, the PP and *La Vanguardia, that* was a historical moment, a historical turning point in which Spain had definitely regenerated and shed its obscure past, this 'sublime moment, of great spiritual intensity' was demoted to the level of a 'circus'.

---

[1] This analysis is not reduced to its syntagmatic aspect – to the chronological succession of functions. It will be complemented by the application of other theories for a more comprehensive description of the construction of the identity of the characters of the narrative. From a formalist perspective, for Propp,

the will of personages, their intentions, cannot be considered as an essential motif for their definition. The important thing is not what they want to do, nor how they feel, but their deeds as such, evaluated and defined from the viewpoint of their meaning for the hero and for the course of the action (Propp, 1984: 81).

It is significant that he called each structural section of the tales a 'function' since his objective was to study what the characters *do* rather than what they *are*.

The present study, focused on collective identities, is heavy dependant on what Propp discards as unimportant for his study: the will, intentions, feelings etc, of the collective characters. The thesis on which this book is based made use of Greimas's analytical apparatus for that purpose. Greimas, as a semanticist is not only interested in *how* meaning is constructed in texts, but also *what* texts mean. The concepts of 'competence' (1989:11), and 'veridiction' (1987:110) are his main contribution to narrative theory and a very important inspiration for this analysis. However, for the sake of clarity, I have decided to keep his theoretical apparatus to a minimum.

[2] All quotes from newspapers in this chapter are from 1996, unless otherwise specified.

[3] 'Carpetovetonic': the *carpetos* and the *vetones* were two Iberian peoples which inhabited part of Central Spain. This adjective has come to encapsulate all the values of Eternal Spain.

[4] Baltasar Porcel's words echo the term 'convivència' (see chapter 2) and its associated values of tolerance and democracy.

[5] It should be noted that the call for a spirit of consensus in the name of democracy or the good functioning of the State, is not a unusual political strategy. In 1993, when the PP was strengthening its attacks on the PSOE, the Socialists suggested the creation of an atmosphere of consensus under the banner of the 'democratic impulse' ('impulso democrático').

[6] The literal Spanish term is a sporting expression: 'to sweat one's shirt'. Although the English translation does not have a sporting ring to it, it keeps the idea of endurance and the possibility of improvement at the end of a process.

[7] Vidal-Quadras was the President of the Catalan PP at the time of the negotiations. His anti-nationalist stance converted him into the main 'enemy' of the Catalan nationalists and his political beheading was demanded as one of the conditions for the pact.

[8] 'reams from Salamanca' refers to the documents of the Second Republic dealing with Catalonia, kept in the archives in Salamanca. They are claimed back by the Catalan Government, the *Generalitat de Catalunya*.

[9] The supposedly commercial Catalan attitude has led them to be compared to the Phoenicians, one of whose most important colonies was precisely in present-day Catalonia.

[10]Calling Catalonia a country ('país') is a common fact in Catalonia. In the rest of Spain it is almost un-heard of. And it is more or less anathema within the Right, which feels more at ease referring to it with the geographical and politically old-fashioned term of 'región'.

[11]A 'tertulia' refers to the very popular radio chat shows in which all types of issues are discussed, the most controversial ones being political. Some of these 'tertulias', particularly those aired on the COPE (the radio station owned partly by the Catholic Church and derogatorily called 'the radio of the bishops') were accused of orchestrating a campaign against the PSOE and their political partners CiU between 1993 and 1996. As far as the attacks against CiU were concerned, they were widely interpreted in Catalonia as attacks against Catalonia herself. The term 'tertuliero' does not exist in Spanish, 'tertuliano', 'contertulio' or 'miembro de la tertulia' being the appropriate word. The ending '-iero' of this made-up word gives it a pejorative and derogatory sense.

[12] 'las cavernarias andadas', translated here as 'the primitive old ways' includes two interesting points. On the one hand, 'the old ways' ('las andadas') refers to the method or approach in which Eternal Spain has always done things: always causing havoc. On the other hand, the term 'cavernarias' (translated here as 'primitive') is related to 'la caverna' (the cavern), that mythical place where, according to Catalan nationalists, Eternal Spain comes from and belongs in.

[13]This prospective knowledge at times looked to historical facts for support. Baltasar Porcel, in yet another use of the myth of the cave, compares (exaggeratedly!) the new elections with those of 1931. On that occasion, the Left Wing coalition, Frente Popular, won with an electoral programme that advocated liberal ideas and the de-centralization of the State. That victory paved the way to the Second Republic. Porcel stated that 'at that

time, a new Spain was also accepted, however there was soon a return to the ferocities of the cave', obviously referring to the Civil War (*La Vanguardia*, 17 March 1996).

[14]Don Pelayo (who died in 737) was elected King of Asturias after the Battle of Covadonga (718) against the Muslims. That victory, attributed to divine protection, did not have the dimensions given to it by legend, but meant the first great defeat of Islam, and has been accepted as the beginning of the Christian Reconquest. The reference to the Civil Wars hints at two supposedly embedded features of Spanishness: the tendency to fight instead of negotiating, and (consequently) the lack of cohesion that keeps Spanish society constantly divided.

[15] My cautious comparison is totally accepted by many analysts. For instance, Josep Maria Ainaud de Lasarte, who has been a member of the Catalan parliament and Barcelona Councillor for CiU, establishes a clear link between the interventionist and 'modernizing' spirit of La Lliga Catalanista and Catalans in general. He sees this spirit in Cambó in the first quarter of the 20th century, in the Catalan ministers during the Franco regime, and in the many Catalan ministers and collaborators with the Central Governments all along the present democratic period. This interesting argument is clearly explained in Ainaud de Lasarte, J. M. (1996).

CHAPTER 4

CONCLUSION

1. National Narratives: Opposition and Consensus

In *The Postmodern Condition: a Report on Knowledge* (1984), Lyotard uses the word postmodern to 'designate the state of our culture following the transformations which, since the end of the nineteenth century, have altered the game rules for science, literature and the arts' (Lyotard, 1984: xxiii). His main claim is that postmodernism is about an 'incredulity towards narratives' (*ibid*: xxiv). Although Lyotard's particular focus is on the function of narratives in the legitimation of scientific knowledge, his claims can be extended to any field of culture (he explicitly mentions 'literature and the arts' in the quotation above). He states that 'the narrative function is losing its functors, its great hero, its great dangers, its great voyages, its great goal' (*ibid*: xxiv). Lyotard announces 'the obsolescence of the metanarrative apparatus of legitimation' (*ibid*: xxiv). This statement implies 'the break up of Grand Narratives' (*ibid*), that is, of totalizing thought systems such as Marxism, Liberalism or Christianity. According to Lyotard, the result of this postmodern condition is that 'the old poles of attraction represented by nation-states, parties, professions, institutions, and historical traditions are losing their attraction ... identifying with the great names, the heroes of contemporary history, is becoming more and more difficult' (Lyotard, 1984: 14).

However, throughout this book it has been shown that the nation and national identity have not been superseded. On the contrary, as Smith points out, of all the collective identities in which human beings share today, national identity is perhaps the most fundamental (Smith, 1991: 143). The persistence of the national frame of identification is particularly true of Spain, where the debate on national identity (which pervades Spanish politics) is one of the problems most resistant to solution – even after the 1978 Constitution and its effort to integrate the peripheral nationalisms.

In this book, it has also been shown that the formulation of national identities in the form of Grand Narratives is strong in Spain. The analyses in chapter 2 and 3 have revealed that different discourses on national identity that crisscross Spanish society segment Spanish reality into collective subjects (the unified Spain, the Two Spains,

Catalonia–Spain). It has been seen how these discourses compete with each other in a way that varies depending on the political circumstances. In moments of political turmoil between all-Spanish parties and peripheral nationalisms (as in the period between 1993–1996), conceptions of national identity in Spain and Catalonia are worlds apart and they relate in a way that is agonistic, based on 'moves' and 'countermoves' (Lyotard, 1984: 16).

In those circumstances, Spanish society becomes constructed following the logic of binarism. From an all-Spanish perspective, the myth of 'The Two Spains' (epitomizing the struggle for the conceptions of Spain between the Conservative Right and the Liberal Left) regains strength. From a peripheral point of view, the opposition between Catalan and Spanish identities is brought to the fore. One might say, with Barthes, that these binary patterns are a reflection of a 'human tendency to categorize experience in terms of dichotomous contrast' (Barthes: 1984: 142). However, binarism has been seen as just *one* possible ideological manner of organizing constructions of society. Indeed, a situation of bipolarity, ungradable opposition and irreconcilability can be developed in the direction of mutual recognition.

That was the case in the coverage of the 2002 Football World Cup, which took place against the background of the relative political and regional calm produced by the pact between the PP and CiU. At that time, the identification of 'us' with the Spanish national team, that is, the metonymy 'one nation, one team' (strongly associated to Francoism in the politically turbulent 1994), was not frowned upon anymore (except in *Avui*). In 2002, the myth of the Two Spains all but disappeared from *El País* and was not present in *El Mundo*. *Avui*, more concerned with the politics of difference between Spain and Catalonia, refused to leave its policy of ungradable opposition and maintained its construction of Spain as stuck in the Francoist past – as opposed to a modern and democratic Catalonia.

The coverage of the pact between CiU and the PP in *La Vanguardia* (studied in Chapter 3) was a clear example of a change from opposition to mutual recognition in a very short period of time. In order to preserve the legitimacy of CiU in an agreement with the until then 'arch-enemy' of the coalition and of Catalonia, *La Vanguardia* (as media outlet of moderate differential Catalanism) constructed the negotiations as a process of justified gradability between the positions of both parties. The justification was presented in the shape of narrative sequences. Along these sequences, the Catalanists explained away their new course of action towards a pact on the grounds of values which, in Catalonia, are generally accepted as part and parcel of the Catalan identity: pactism, self-sacrificial sense of state, moderation, responsibility.

Amongst the sequences of the narrative, the test was of utmost importance. That test, set by the Catalanists to the PP, established a deal which could be worded in simple terms as: in order to have our parliamentary support, you have to change your mentality, you have to acquire the right knowledge about what Catalonia really is, and about the plurinational, plurilingual and pluricultural nature of Spain.

In the successful interpretation of the test, the Partido Popular proved a kind of 'ideological becoming' (Bakhtin, 1981: 341). That is, they had *learned* and improved. As a consequence, a new space, shared by Spain and Catalonia, was made possible. This common space referred to the almost mythical *encaix* of Catalonia in Spain, the new stable space where Catalonia could comfortably fit in. Two alternative interpretations of the events tried to de-legitimize the whole process. One of them established that the PP had deceived Catalonia (at times with the complicity of CiU); for the other, the Eternal Spain of the PP had not passed the test, nothing had been learned.

2. National Pedagogy and Renewal

Beneath the idea of lack of knowledge lay the idea of the possibility of transformation and redemption. As John Fiske observes:

> Anthropologically, Propp's schema tells the archetypal story of the young male's acceptance into maturity and society; marriage is the achievement of individual maturity and the insertion of that mature person into a network of social roles and obligations ... In such an explanation of Propp's structure, the struggle between the hero and the villain is a metaphorical transformation of that between the forces of order and those of disorder, good and evil, or culture and nature. Such a struggle is fundamental in all societies, and the narrative explores the role of human and social agents in it (Fiske, 1987: 138).

The last point to be discussed in this book is precisely the possibility of transformation and redemption of Spain, which echoes the mythical passage from nature to civilization, or the conversion of a character from being Dionysian to being Apollonian.

It has been seen that for Catalanists, the Apollonian character is the Catalan society, constructed as having a type of identity typically ruled by obligation and knowledge – 'what the Apollonian subject wants is determined by the knowledge of things and situations; it is the subject subjected to the norms it knows' (Blanco and Bueno, 1980: 105). It was seen in Chapter 3 that a sense of duty and rational responsibility was presented as a constituent feature of Catalan identity. The PP (as the representative of Eternal Spain) was Dionysian on account of their denial of 'a certain type of rationality' (*ibid*: 104) and moderation. It was the supposed lack of a habit of normal dialogue and consensus that made the columnist of *La Vanguardia*, Baltasar Porcel, represent the PP as 'trouble maker' ('bronco' in the Spanish original) (*La Vanguardia*, 14 March 1994). And that imposition of will without any type of thoughtful reflection made the same author depict the PP as a dogmatic character that understands 'Spanishness as a sect, and not as a whole agreed by consensus' (*La Vanguardia*, 24 March 1994).

The idea of an Apollonian and civilizing Catalonia was expressed by Oriol Pi de Cabanyes, who stated that 'pactism has taught us ... that the best policy is the one that civilizes the opposite' (*La Vanguardia*, 7 March 1994). Moreover, the possible transformation of the PP was coded by the same columnist as a transition from the savage state to the state of civilization in an article quoted in Chapter 3: 'Aznar has a great opportunity. But he must know that absolutism is still waiting to be *tamed in the mind*' (*La Vanguardia*, 7 March 1994, my italics). Four days earlier the same journalist stated: 'we might be starting a slow transition towards a plural Spain. But in this issue the role of *culture* cannot be underestimated' (*La Vanguardia*, 3 March, 1994, my italics). And after the PP supposedly started to give the first signs of accepting the Catalanist values, Baltasar Porcel observed, in one of his opinion columns, that 'the fact that the Right deny their own values might open a thoroughfare of concord and finally of civilization' (*La Vanguardia*, 11 March 1994).

Because of this emphasis on civilization, culture and knowledge, the representation of the relationship of Spain with Catalonia carried out in *La Vanguardia* was almost invariably educational or didactic. This type of relationship logically implies that

Catalonia and the Spain to be taught and civilized are not equal. Furthermore, didactics, as Lyotard points out, implies three presuppositions that were present in the narrative representation of the events analysed in chapter 3: 'the addressee' (that is, Partido Popular in this narrative), 'the student, does not know what the sender' (CiU in our case) 'knows: obviously, that is why he has something to learn'. Lyotard continues:

> Its second presupposition is that the student can learn what the sender knows and become an expert whose competence is equal to that of his master. This double requirement supposes a third: that there are statements for which the exchange of arguments and the production of proof constituting the pragmatics of research are considered to have been sufficient, and which can therefore be transmitted through teaching as they stand, in the guise of indisputable truths (Lyotard, 1984: 25).

The value system of the educator is based on truth. And that is exactly what was seen in chapter 3. The dynamics of the narrative aimed at the conversion of Eternal Spain from its own false value system (based on the idea that Spain is homogeneous) to the opposing legitimate one (based on the conception of a pluralist, democratic and European Spain). The glorification of the PP, both after the 1996 and 2000 elections, meant that the student had become as competent as the master and could be seen on an equal footing.

The representation of relationship between Spain and Catalonia as pedagogical was not at all new to this period. As the Spanish historian Javier Tusell observes, as early as 1916 one of the intellectual fathers of Catalan nationalism, Prat de la Riba, recommended the Catalanist politician Cambó 'to explain Catalanist ideas in the rest of Spain' (Tusell, 1998: 24). Nowadays, it is relatively normal for Catalanist politicians to embark on similar 'explanatory' missions in Spain (mainly Madrid). This attitude was reproduced by Oriol Pi de Cabanyes who stated that 'we [Catalans] have the historical opportunity to make the PP understand what Catalonia is ... we have to do a lot of pedagogical work (*La Vanguardia*, 25 March 1994). The same columnist quoted Josep Piqué (who would later become a member of PP, then its political spokesperson and then minister of various portfolios), reminding of the necessity of introducing the culture of pactism: '[t]here is here a pedagogical task to be carried out by the political class' (*La Vanguardia*, 21 March).

This pedagogical attitude is not particular to Catalan nationalism but belongs to all intellectuals of all convictions attempting to renew Spain. It was seen in Chapter 1 how the dictatorship of Primo de Rivera was guided by a type of right wing regenerationism, two of the founding ideals of which were the possibility of change of Spanish cultural and political life, and the essential role of education in the transformation of the country. As far as the liberal regenerationist intellectuals were concerned, they erected themselves as 'the educators of the nation" (Graham and Labanyi, 1996: 127), and consequently embarked on a civilizing mission based on the upgrading of the educational level of the population understood not only in the technical sense but also as a 'special ethos ... that tried to pave the way for the progress of mankind' (Castañón Rodríguez, 1998). Miguel de Unamuno, for instance, 'took part in that spiritual renovation of Spain, understood as a pedagogical mission' (*ibid*). The other main figure of liberal regenerationism, Ortega y Gasset, adopted a tutoring attitude which can be summed up by the ideal ruling *El Sol*, a liberal newspaper whose objective was 'to educate readers in the complexity of the society in which they lived and thus to encourage them to support or promote the reforms necessary for the country's modernization' (Montero, 1996: 127). This generation was guided by a positive belief in the redemption of Spain via education, based on the idea that if 'education makes the man' then 'national characters can also be modified' (García de Cortázar and González, 1994: 401).

The ideal of the regeneration and redemption of Spain and the transformation of its 'national character' has also been a key element in the analysis of the 1994 Football World Cup in Chapter 2. The unitarian discourse promoted a concept of Spanish national identity which was regarded by liberal and peripheral discourses as centralist, un-civilized, conservative and old-fashioned. As far as the Spanish liberal ideology (of *El País* and some articles of *El Mundo*) is concerned, Chapter 2 has showed the importance that it places on intellectualism and culture in the regeneration of the country. However the divisive myth of the Two Spains was still presented in 1994 as strong enough to prevent any real regeneration of conservative Spain and of Spain as a whole. Contrary to the idea that this division has died out (which prevailed during the transition to democracy), columnists such as Vázquez Montalbán (*El País*) continued to exploit this ideological segmentation of Spanish society in order to de-legitimize the political aspirations and actions of the Right (or Centre–Right) as represented by the PP. The same segmentation was used by

Francisco Umbral (*El Mundo*), in order to de-legitimize the power of the PSOE. For its part, the disjunctive Catalanist discourse of *Avui* ridiculed any attempt at the regeneration of Spain, undoubtedly because a regenerated Spain would render more radical version of Catalanist nationalism politically irrelevant.

In 2002, at the time of the Football World Cup, analysis of media coverage of the event showed that, with the exception of *Avui* (heavily focused on regional differences and the presentation of Spain as stuck in the past), all the newspapers analysed had moved to a kind of territorial agreement and a celebration of the status quo – a situation which favoured the use (in all dailies, including *La Vanguardia*) of a language normally related to Spanish nationalism in 1994. However, at the risk of sounding like a visionary, one can easily imagine that given the right (or wrong) twist of circumstances, controversy between Catalonia and Spain could come to the fore again and society become presented as divided and fragmented. The immediate past of agreement and harmony could be readily forgotten and the ghost of the Francoist past dusted down again as a de-legitimizing tool. In Catalonia, Spain could become generally regarded again as a villainous, ungrateful and primitive State (and society) that suffocates industrious, moderate, modern, European Catalonia. A never ending process that will keep Spanish and Catalan identities forever undefined and forever controversial.

APPENDIX

BNG. Bloque Nacionalista Galego. Left-wing nationalist party of Galicia.

CC. Coalición Canaria. Centre–right coalition of nationalist/regionalist parties of the Canary Islands.

CiU. Convergència i Unió. This Catalanist coalition, led by Jordi Pujol, is formed by Convergència democràtica de Catalunya and Unió democràtica. It has been in power in Catalonia since the first elections to the *Generalitat* (Catalan Autonomous Government) in 1980. Since 1993 it has also played a major role in all-Spanish politics after its support for the PSOE (between 1993 and 1996) and for the PP (between 1996 until present).

EA. Eusko Alkartasuna was formed in 1986 by dissident members of the PNV (Partido Nacionalista Vasco).

ERC. Esquerra Republicana de Catalunya. Republican, left wing and pro-independence catalanist party.

HB. Herri Batasuna. This Basque left wing, pro-independence party is widely regarded as ETA's political wing.

IU. Izquierda Unida is a coalition of left-wing parties whose core is the PCE, the Spanish Communist Party. In Catalonia, this coalition is called **IU–IC**, Izquierda Unida – Inciativa per Catalunya.

PNV. Partido Nacionalista Vasco. This centre–right nationalist party is the dominant political force in the Basque Country.

PP. Partido Popular. It was founded as Alianza Popular in 1976 by the post-francoist section of the political spectrum, led by Francoist minister Manuel Fraga. In 1989 José María Aznar became the leader of the party. Under his leadership, the PP underwent a shift towards the centre. After this renovation, the PP obtained successive victories in municipal, European, regional and, eventually, national elections in 1996 and 2000.

PSOE. Partido Socialista Obrero Español was founded in 1879 and played a major role in the Second Republic in the 1930s. Due to internal strife, it had relatively little importance in the anti-Franco opposition. The PSOE underwent essential political renovation in the early 1970s, effectively becoming a social democratic party. Thanks to this move towards the centre, the socialists obtained an overwhelming victory in 1982 under the leadership of Felipe González. They stayed in power until 1996.

U V. Unió Valenciana. Centre–right regionalist party of the Autonomous Community of Valencia.

BIBLIOGRAPHY

Abrams, D., Hogg, M. (eds.) *Social Identity Theory: Constructive and Critical Advances*, London, Harvester Wheatsheaf, 1990.

Ainaud de Lasarte, J. M., *Ministros catalanes en Madrid*, Barcelona, Planeta, 1996.

Alcoba López, A., *Deporte y comunicación*, Madrid, Caja de Ahorros y Monte de Piedad de Madrid, 1987.

Anderson, B., *Imagined Communities: Reflections on the Origin and Spread of Nationalism*, London, Verso, 1983.

Aristotle, *De Poetica*, in Ross W. D. (ed.) *The Works of Aristotle*, vol XI, Oxford, Oxford University Press, 1924.

Asa Berger, A., *Narratives in Popular Culture, Media, and Everyday Life*, London, Sage Publications, 1997.

Bakhtin M., 'Discourse in the Novel' in Holquist M. (ed.) *The Dialogic Imagination: four essays*, Austin, University of Texas, 1981.

Balfour, S., 'The Loss of the Empire, Regenerationism, and the Forging of a Myth of National Identity' in Graham, H., Labanyi, J. (eds.) *Spanish Cultural Studies: An Introduction: The Struggle for Modernity*, (Oxford, Oxford University Press, 1996) pp. 25–31.

Barthes, R., *Mythologies*, London, Jonathan Cape, 1972.

Barthes, R., *Writing Degree Zero & Elements of Semiology*, London, Jonathan Cape, 1984.

Barthes, R., *Image, Music, Text*, Glasgow, Fontana Press, 1987.

Benveniste, E., *Problems in General Linguistics*, Florida, University of Miami Press, 1971.

Bignell, J., *Media Semiotics: An Introduction*, Manchester, Manchester University Press, 1987.

Blain, N., Boyle, R., O'Donnell, H., *Sport and National Identity in the European Media*, Leicester, Leicester University Press, 1993.

Blanco F., Bueno R., *La metodología del análisis semiótico*, Lima, Universidad de Lima, 1980.

Bourdieu, P., *On Television and Journalism*, London, Pluto Press, 1996.

Cardús, S., *Política de paper: premsa i poder a Catalunya, 1981–1992*, Barcelona, Edicions La Campana, 1995.

Castañón Rodríguez, J., *El lenguaje periodístico del fútbol*, Valladolid, Universidad de Valladolid, 1993.

Castañón Rodríguez, J., *El deporte moderno y Unamuno*, El País Digital, 1998.

Eco, U., *Signo*, Barcelona, Labor, 1994.

Elias, N., Dunning, E., *Quest for Excitement: Sport and Leisure in the Civilizing Process*, Oxford, Blackwell, 1993.

Fernández, F., Mercadé, F., Oltra, B., *Once tesis sobre la cuestión nacional de España*, Barcelona, Anthropos, 1983.

Fishman, J. A., *Language and Ethnicity in Minority Sociolinguistic Perspective*, Avon, Multilingual Matters, 1989.

Fiske, J., *Television Culture: Popular Pleasures and Politics*, London, Methuen, 1987.

Forgacs, D. (ed.), *Gramsci: A Reader*, London, Lawrence and Wishart, 1988.

Fowler, R., *Language in the News: Discourse and Ideology in the Press*, London, Routledge, 1991.

Fox, I., *La invención de España: nacionalismo liberal e identidad nacional*, Madrid, Cátedra, 1997.

García de Cortázar, F., González Vesga, J.M., *Breve historia de España*, Madrid, Alianza Editorial, 1994.

Gil-Calvo, E., Ortiz, J., Revuelta, M., *Repensar la prensa*, Madrid, Debate, 2002.

Gastil, J., 'Undemocratic Discourse: a Review of Theory and Research on Political Discourse', *Discourse & Society*, 3:4 (1992), pp. 469–500.

Graham, H., 'Popular Culture in the Years of Hunger', in Graham, H. and Labanyi, J. (eds.) *Spanish Cultural Studies: An Introduction: The Struggle for Modernity* (Oxford, Oxford University Press, 1996), pp. 237–245.

Graham, H. and Labanyi, J., 'Élites in Crisis: 1898–1931' in Graham, H. and Labanyi, J. (eds.), *Spanish Cultural Studies: An Introduction: The Struggle for Modernity* (Oxford, Oxford University Press, 1996), pp. 21–23.

Graham, H. and Labanyi, J. (eds.), *Spanish Cultural Studies: An Introduction: The Struggle for Modernity*, Oxford, Oxford University Press, 1996.

Graham, H. and Labanyi, J., 'Culture and Modernity: The Case of Spain' in Graham, H. and Labanyi, J. (eds.), *Spanish Cultural Studies: An Introduction: The Struggle for Modernity* (Oxford, Oxford University Press, 1996), pp. 1–19.

Graham, H. and Sánchez, A., 'The Politics of 1992' in Graham, H. and Labanyi, J. (eds.), *Spanish Cultural Studies: An Introduction: The Struggle for Modernity* (Oxford, Oxford University Press, 1996), pp. 406–418.

Gramsci, A., *Selections From the Prison Notebooks*, London, Laurence and Whishart, 1971.

Greimas, A. J., *En torno al sentido: ensayos semióticos*, Madrid, Fragua, 1973.

Greimas, A.J., *La semiótica del texto: ejercicios prácticos,* Barcelona, Paidós, 1976.

Greimas, A. J., *Semiótica y ciencias sociales*, Madrid, Fragua, 1980.

Greimas, A. J. *On meaning: Selected Writings in Semiotic Theory*, London, France Pinter Publishers, 1987.

Greimas, A. J., *Del sentido II,* Madrid, Editorial Gredos, 1989.

González Antón, L., *España y las Españas*, Madrid, Alianza Editorial, 1997.

Halliday, M. A. K., *Language as Social Semiotic: The Social Interpretation of Language and Meaning*, London, Eduard Arnold, 1979.

Hobsbawm, E. 'Inventing Traditions' in Hobsbawn, E. and Ranger T. (eds.) *The Invention of Tradition*, (Cambridge, Cambridge University Press, 1992) pp. 1–14.

Hobsbawm, E., *Nations and Nationalism since 1780: Programme, Myth, Reality*, Cambridge, Cambridge University Press, 1990.

Hodge, R., Kress, G., *Language as Ideology*, London, Routledge, 1993.

Hogg M.A., McGarthy C., 'Self-categorization and Social Identity', in Abrams, D., Hogg, M. (eds.) *Social Identity Theory: Constructive and Critical Advances*, (London, Harvester Wheatsheaf, 1990) pp. 10–27.

Hooper, J., *The Spaniards: a Portrait of the New Spain*, London, Penguin Books, 1987.

Hopkin, J., 'An Incomplete alternation: the Spanish Elections of March 1996', *International Journal of Iberian Studies*, 9:2 (1996), pp. 110–116.

Jameson, F., *The Prison-House of Language: A Critical Account of Structuralism and Russian Formalism*, Princeton, Princeton University Press, 1974.

Johnson L. and Hewstone M., 'Intergroup Contact: Social Identity and Social Cognition', in Abrams, D., Hogg, M. (eds.) *Social Identity Theory: Constructive and Critical Advances*, (Harvester Wheatsheaf, London, 1990) pp. 185–210.

Keating, M., *State and Regional Nationalism: Territorial Politics and the European State*, London, Haverster, 1988.

Kremnitz, G., *Multilingualisme Social*, Barcelona, Edicions 62, 1992 (first published in 1990 as *Gesellschaftliche Mehrsprachigkeit*, Wilhelm Braumüller Universität Verlagscuchhandlung, Viena).

Kuper, S., *Football Against the Enemy*, London, Orion, 1994.

Labanyi, J. (1996) 'Postmodernism and the Problem of Cultural Identity' in Graham, H. and Labanyi, J. (eds.) *Spanish Cultural Studies: An Introduction: The Struggle for Modernity*, Oxford, Oxford University Press, 1996, pp. 396–406.

Lawlor T. and Rigby M., *Contemporary Spain: Essays and Texts on Politics, Economics, Education and Employment, and Society*, London, Longman, 1998.

León Solís, F., 'Transition(s) to Democracy and Discourses of Memory', *International Journal of Iberian Studies*, 16: 1, 2003.

León Solís, F., 'El juego de las nacionalidades: discursos de identidad nacional española', *International Journal of Iberian Studies*, 9:1, (1996), pp. 28–45.

León Solís, F., 'Cataluña: víctima y redentora de España' *International Journal of Iberian Studies*, 11:3 (1998), pp. 156–165.

León Solís, F. and O'Donnell, H. (1994), *The Catalan Janus: Discourses of National Identity in the Catalan Press*, paper delivered at the First Scottish Conference of Catalan Studies, Strathclyde University.

Lévi-Strauss, C., *The Savage Mind*, London, Weidenfeld and Nicolson, 1974.

London, J., 'The Ideology and Practice of Sport' in Graham, H. and Labanyi, J. (eds.) *Spanish Cultural Studies: An Introduction: The Struggle for Modernity* (Oxford, Oxford University Press, 1996), pp. 204–207.

Longhurst, A., 'Culture and Development: the Impact of the 1960s 'desarrollismo' in Jordan, B. and Morgan-Tamosunas, R. (eds.) *Contemporay Spanish Cultural Studies* (London, Arnold, 2000) pp. 17–28.

Lozano J., Peña-Marín, C., Abril, G., *Análisis del discurso: hacia una semiótica de la interacción textual*, Madrid, Cátedra, 1993.

Lyons J., *Semantics: vol.I*, Cambridge, Cambridge University Press, 1977a.

Lyons J., *Semantics: vol.II*, Cambridge, Cambridge University Press, 1977b.

Lyotard, J-F., *The Postmodern Condition: A Report on Knowledge*, Manchester, Manchester University Press, 1984.

Mar-Molinero, C., 'Catalan' in Rodgers, E. (ed.) *Encyclopedia of Contemporary Spanish Culture* (London, Routledge, 1999), p. 90.

Medina, J., *L'Anticatalanisme del diari Abc: (1916–1936)*, Barcelona, Abadía de Montserrat, 1995.

Moliner, M., *Diccionario de Uso del Español*: vol. 1, Madrid, Editorial Gredos, 1990a.

Moliner, M., *Diccionario de Uso del Español*: vol. 2, Madrid, Editorial Gredos, 1990b.

Montero, E., 'Reform Idealized: The Intellectual and Ideological Origins of the Second Republic' in Graham, H. and Labanyi, J. (eds.) *Spanish Cultural Studies: An Introduction: The Struggle for Modernity* (Oxford, Oxford University Press, 1996) pp. 124–133.

Montero, R., Political Transition and Cultural Democracy: Coping with the Speed of Change in Graham, H. and Labanyi, J. (eds.) *Spanish Cultural Studies: An Introduction: The Struggle for Modernity*, Oxford, Oxford University Press, 1996), pp. 315–320.

Morón Arroyo, C., *El "alma de España": Cien años de inseguridad*, Oviedo, Ediciones Nobel, 1996.

O'Donnell, H., 'Mapping the mythical: a Geopolitics of National Sporting Stereotypes', *Discourse & Society*, 5:3 (1994), London, Sage, pp. 345–380.

O'Donnell, H., 'Abc' in Rodgers, E. (ed.) *Encyclopedia of Contemporary Spanish Culture* (London, Routledge, 1999), p. 2

O'Donnell, H., 'Avui' in Rodgers, E. (ed.) *Encyclopedia of Contemporary Spanish Culture* (London, Routledge, 1999), pp. 40–41.

O'Donnell, H., 'El Mundo' in Rodgers, E. (ed.) *Encyclopedia of Contemporary Spanish Culture* (London, Routledge, 1999), pp. 352–353.

O'Donnell, H., 'El País' in Rodgers, E. (ed.) *Encyclopedia of Contemporary Spanish Culture* (London, Routledge, 1999), pp. 386–387.

O'Donnell, H., 'La Vanguardia' in Rodgers, E. (ed.) *Encyclopedia of Contemporary Spanish Culture* (London, Routledge, 1999), pp. 538–539.

Ortega y Gasset, J., *Obras completas: vol. 1*, Madrid, Revista de Occidente, 1946.

Ortega y Gasset, J., *La rebelión de las* masas, Barcelona, Circulo de Lectores, 1983.

Pérez Vejo, T., *Nación, identidad nacional y otros mitos nacionalistas*, Madrid, Nobel, 1990.

Pi, R., Pujol J., *Cataluña, España*, Barcelona, Espasa, 1996.

Prat de la Riba, E., *La nacionalidad catalana*, Madrid, Biblioteca Nueva, 1998.

Preston, P., 'El discreto encanto del general Franco', *Acis*, 4:1 (1991), p. 173.

Propp, V., *Morphology of the Folktale*, University of Texas Press, Austin.

Reigosa, C. G. (ed.), *El Idioma español en el deporte*, Madrid, Colección comunicación y lenguaje, Fundación EFE, 1994.

Reis, C. A. dos, *Towards a Semiotics of ideology*, Berlin, Mouton de Gruyter, 1993.

Ringrose M., Learner, A. (eds.), *Reimagining the Nation*, Buckingham, Open University Press, 1993.

Rivière, M., *El problema: Madrid–Barcelona*, Madrid, Ediciones Temas de Hoy, 1996.

Rodgers, E., 'The Reyes Católicos and "National Unity": Aspects of Nationalist Historiography in Post-Civil War Spain', *International Journal of Iberian Studies*, 7:2 (1994), pp. 53–59.

Rodgers, E., 'Falange' in Rodgers, E. (ed.) *Encyclopedia of Contemporary Spanish Culture* (London, Routledge, 1999), p. 173.

Rowe, D., 'Modes of Sports Writing', in Dahlgren, P. and Sparks, C. (eds.) *Journalism and Popular Culture*, (London, Sage, 1996), pp. 96–111.

Sahagún, F., 'La Transformación de España: España fin de siglo: 1975–2000' in *Anuario de los temas y los protagonistas 2000* (Barcelona, Planeta-de Agostini, 2001), pp. 378–379.

Schlesinger, P., *Media, State and Nation: Political Violence and Collective Identities*, London, Sage, 1991.

Shaw, D., *Fútbol y franquismo*, Madrid, Alianza Editorial, 1987.

Smith, A., *National Identity*, London, Peguin Books, 1991.

Smith, A., 'The Nation: Invented, Imagined, Reconstructed' in Ringrose, M. and Learner, A., (eds.) *Reimagining the Nation* (Buckingham, Open University Press, 1993), pp. 9–28.

Strinati, D., *An Introduction to Theories of Popular Culture*, London, Routledge, London, 2000.

Terry, A., 'Catalan Literary Modernisme and Noucentisme: From Dissidence to Order' in Graham, H. and Labanyi, J. (eds.) *Spanish Cultural Studies: An Introduction: The Struggle for Modernity*, (Oxford, Oxford University Press, 1996), pp. 55–57.

Terry, A., 'Foix, J.V', in Rodgers, E. (ed.) *Encyclopedia of Contemporary Spanish Culture* (London, Routledge, 1999), pp. 192–193.

Thompson, J. B., *Ideology and Modern Culture*, Cambridge, Polity Press, 1990.

Trudgill, P., *Sociolinguistics: An Introduction to Language and Society*, London, Penguin Books, 1993.

Tusell, J., 'Introducción: Prat de la Riba y "La nacionalitat catalana"' in Prat de la Riba, E., *La Nacionalidad Catalana* (Madrid, Biblioteca Nueva, 1998).

Ucelay de Cal, E., 'The Nationalists of the Periphery: Culture and Politics in the Construction of National Identity' in Graham, H. and Labanyi, J. (eds.) *Spanish Cultural Studies: An Introduction: The Struggle for Modernity*, (Oxford, Oxford University Press, 1996), pp. 32–39.

Unamuno, M. de, *Obras Completas: vol. III*, ed. García Blanco, M., Barcelona, Vergara, 1958.

Unamuno, M. de, *Obras Completas: vol. IX: Discursos y Artículos*, ed. García Blanco, M., Madrid, Escélicer, 1971.

Van Dijk, T. A., *News as Discourse*, Hillsdale, New Jersey, Lawrence Erlbaum Associates, 1988.

Vázquez Montalbán, M., 'Pròleg: el Barça: de la guerra civil a la casa reial' in Burns Marañón, J., *Barça: La passió d'un poble* (Barcelona, Anagrama, 1999) pp. 5–10.

Verdú, V., *El fútbol: mitos, ritos y símbolos*, Madrid, Alianza Editorial, 1980.

Verón, E., *La semiosis social: fragmentos de una teoría de la discursividad*, Barcelona, Gedisa, 1998.

INDEX

A

B

P

R

S

V

Vázquez Montalbán, M.	7, 44, 55, 58-60, 63-65, 75, 78, 145
Verdú, Vicente	48, 51
victimism	55, 59
Vidal-Quadras	114, 138
Vila-Matas, Enrique	78

W/Z

wedding	see marriage
Wimbledon Tennis Championship	49
World Cup 1994	6, 28, 39, 41, 46-76
World Cup 2002	9, 75, 78, 141
Zubizarreta, A.	47